Of Literary Circles and Nightingales

Of Literary Circles and Nightingales

RADKA YAKIMOV

OF LITERARY CIRCLES AND NIGHTINGALES

ISBN-13: 9781523629916
ISBN-10: 1523629916
LCCN: 2016902957
CreateSpace Independent Publishing Platform,
North Charleston, South Carolina

Contents

Prologue · ix

Part One: · 1
    The Literary Circle · 3

Part Two: ·19
    The Fortune-Teller ·21
    The House on the Corner · · · · · · · · · · · · · · · · · ·26
    The Party, the Reluctant Collaborator,
    and the Mad House · 40
    Places to Sleep ·52
    It Is All about "Happy Endings" · · · · · · · · · · · · · ·71
    Moskovska 5 and the Broken Marriage · · · · · · · · · · 80

Part Three: ·93
    A Flash of Memory ·95
    West Berlin and the Convenience of
    Following Orders · 97

Epilogue ·109

Prologue

It was 1995, and I was far away from home. Standing, as I was, on top of Table Mountain and marveling at the ocean waters of the Atlantic and Indian meeting along a distinct line at the tip of the African continent, I was struck by the recollection of an obscure thought I had nurtured once and by the urgent need to redefine it at this moment. As a small child, long ago, and in a place I then called home, I had developed an idea about the exact location of the end of our world. It was Patagonia. Now, looking at the vast ocean panorama from the top of the rocky plateau on a clear, although cheerless, day, I had the strangest sensation that the line of the horizon was not the visual illusion where sky and water meet, but the very edge of the earth. And beyond that was an unimaginable chasm.

It was a startling thought that begged questions. Why at this instant, and why on this particular trip to South Africa, had it come to my mind? And why had it maintained its vividness for so long? In addition to that moment of awareness, many other smaller and not as earth-shattering observations popped into my mind, as fresh as if they had happened yesterday. Perhaps much of it had to do with the apartheid system that held this country in its iron grip until only recently, and the scars it had left, still evident and hard to ignore. Perhaps these had awakened the memories of the past, of another country suffocating in an iron grasp of a different kind not too long ago. Both places filled me with the same mix of emotions, and with an intensity that brought a deluge of images and let painful and confusing thoughts spring forward to weigh on my mind all over again.

We were on our way along the Garden Route in a bus full of tourists. The view from the window, running like scenes of a motion picture, a National Geographic production, varied from simply magnificent to breathtakingly awesome. People spoke in hushed voices, and the clicking of cameras was the dominating noise over the hum of wheels running on asphalt. A few hours after boarding the bus in Cape Town, somewhere during our meanderings inside the interior of the humid and stuffy Van Zyl's Chamber of Cango Caves, Oudtshoorn, while admiring the surreal view of stalactites and stalagmites, the hushed sound of a familiar tongue reached my ears. It was impossible to identify exactly the direction it was coming from or to catch a glimpse of the people communicating in that language. But it put me on guard. Curiosity mixed with the foreboding that one feels when reminded of a dark and secretive world took hold of me in a flash. At the time, there was more than one group of tourists in the caves, and by the end of the tour, and during the following couple of days on the road, overwhelmed by the sights and sounds of magnificent and unique beauty, the incident that had startled me in the Cango Caves receded into my subconscious.

It was in the spacious hall of a hotel in Umtata, lined by long tables spread with the morning breakfast buffet, that I heard the voices from the Cango Caves again. They came from a family of four, two children and two adults—presumably their grandparents—absorbed in conversation regarding the choices one faced with all the display of food as they piled their plates with stuff. It was obvious also that this was indeed a family by the unmistakable affection, care, and indulgence the adults demonstrated toward the young siblings. It was a heartwarming sight I found hard to ignore, but still not enough of an incentive to try to involve myself in a conversation with compatriots left behind long ago. A sense of discomfort took hold of me as I listened to the unsuspecting, like a spy coming in from the cold. So I picked up my plate and carried it to the furthest corner of the room, took a seat at the only empty table I could find, and strategically turned my back to the rest of the room. My companion followed me, taking the seat next to me. And just as I had settled comfortably, a deep male voice speaking in English, with the distinct accent I was so well acquainted with, made me lift my gaze.

"Do you mind if we join you?" the man said.

"By all means." I heard the sound of my voice articulating a reply.

For a while I tried to concentrate on my meal, avoiding any eye contact with the people sharing my table, trying to stop the sound of their conversation from reaching my brain. It did not work.

"Excuse me, but I'd like to introduce myself. My name is…" I blurted in defeat.

After a short and awkward pause, the man raised himself from his chair, proffered his hand, and introduced himself, his wife, and the two children. The wife just smiled; the children stopped their chatter and fixed their eyes on me and my companion. Next to me, my friend was grinning awkwardly, lost in a situation she found herself in unexpectedly.

Earlier that morning, at the urging of the tour guide, the entire group had stepped out to take a look at the blanket of mist covering the earth below. The sky was bright and clear and the air was translucent, reflecting on the surface of the strange, still mass surrounding us like an ocean around an island. We were told that this phenomenon occurs at dawn and lasts until the sun comes up and burns away the mist. It was a memorable sight, a befitting finish for some of the tourists who had reached the end of their trip and were heading back to Cape Town. We, though, were to continue all the way to Johannesburg, through Sabi-Sabi resort, Kruger Park, and other attractions. The family members we met at the dining hall were switching buses and continuing the trip with our group. The initial awkwardness in our interactions remained throughout the entire trip. I kept wondering about the fact that a family of four was able to afford such an exotic trip, even though there was no longer a problem with going abroad. To my way of thinking, it was inconceivable that ordinary citizens of a former communist state would have the means for such a trip. It was hard to miss the caution one detected in their spoken words and the look in their eyes while listening to—rather, hanging on—every word I said in the course of any conversation involving personal history and opinions, inescapable topics when people from a country such as ours meet in such exotic and remote circumstances.

Slowly, the awkward discomfort of the last twenty-four hours turned into a panic: In an instant my thoughts scattered, like a flock of birds perched on a tree suddenly spooked by danger taking off and flying away—frantic. In the face of the older man from the family we shared a table with in the hall of a hotel in Umtata, I recognized a young man from our high school Literary Circle from forty-five years ago. The long years since then had been full of life-changing experiences that clogged my mind, leaving no space for memories of a more distant past of high school and Literary Circles, rendering them too remote and inconsistent with the rest. For, in some respect, those were happy, even hopeful times.

My overblown reaction to this recollection was partially due to the place and the state of my mind, but also on account of a weird coincidence. Shortly before leaving home for the trip to South Africa, I had found an unusual old notebook in a drawer full of memorabilia that I had put away long ago and forgotten about. The design of the notebook's rigid cover, shades of brown and beige flowers scattered on a gray background, did not evoke any memories. The interior sides of the front and back covers were finished in a different type of paper, of low quality but covered by a tasteful pattern of repetitive geometrical forms of different pastel colors. The exposed strip of the block of inside pages was painted a dark rose. There was no sticker on top with a title indicating the contents inside. So I hesitated, partially out of fear that the pages of the book would fall apart once the book was opened, or that the writing would be faded away, which would fill me only with regrets. Well, curiosity prevailed.

Across the first yellowish-brown page, there was a title in big, bold letters: *Journal of the Literary Circle meetings of VIIIA and VIIIB class.* The inside pages were filled with notes written in a familiar handwriting. Mine. This was not a surprise because I had been a member of the Literary Circle and was responsible for keeping the journal, but each entry had to be approved by Comrade[1] Tchalukova, the teacher responsible for organizing and overseeing this extracurricular activity. I suppose Comrade Tchalukova did not keep the journal after the last entry and it remained with me. And in a moment of confusion and tension, Mother must have packed the notebook along with the documents and photos she used to send in trickles throughout the years, taking advantage of good-willed friends and friends of friends traveling across the Iron Curtain.

---

1   Comrade—a title used in an egalitarian, classless socialist state, imposed replacement to the defunct bourgeois "Mr.", "Mrs.", "Miss", "Ms." etc., in a capitalist state.

So I read them, and reread them, and mused over what was written. And I came to the conclusion that this was not exactly the stuff *The Communist Manifesto*[2] was made of, but it was pretty effective, judging by the results. Also, I feel compelled to clarify that the first time I read the journal, some things did not sound so strange to me, but with each subsequent reading they grew weirder and weirder...

But, to paraphrase the highly respected F. Nietzsche, that is a matter of opinion, no?

---

2 *The Communist Manifesto* by Karl Marx and Friedrich Engels, published in 1848.

Part One

The Literary Circle

Journal of the Literary Circle meetings of VIIIA and VIIIB class
General assembly
Plan of items to be discussed

1. The reality reflected in our national literature............. MK
2. The building of socialism reflected in our folk music........ EP
3. Analysis of the works of remarkable Soviet writers:
   a. A. Fadeyev: *The Young Guard*...............................AL
   b. N. Biryukov: *Seagull*......................................DA
   c. M. Gorky: *Collected Works*................................ AA
   d. N. Ostrovsky: *How the Steel Was Tempered*...................AA
   e. B. Gorbatov: *Nepokoryonnye*[3].............................AS

4. Initiative:
   This item of the plan included the staging of a collectively cre-
   ated play: "To Be Vigilant."
   The responsibility for different aspects of the play goes to:
   The idea..AS
   Dialog..AS, EP, AA
   Sketches for the stage setting.......................IG

---

3 *Nepokoryonnye* (Russ.)—"unconquerable."

Follow-up:
The play was presented with great success to the members of the Literary Circle.

Competition for Comrade Stalin's Birthday

Works by members of the Literary Circle of VIIIA and VIIIB class submitted in the competition:
"The Great Stalin Is with Us!" short story by AS
"Happiness," short story by EP
"Stalin," poem by RG

December 18, 1951
A celebratory meeting of the Literary Circle in honor of Comrade Stalin

Today, December 18, 1951, the cold winter sun seems to be sending special smiles to the members of the Literary Circle in a hurry to their school. Will you be surprised indeed what this enthusiasm is for? Is it possible that you don't know? Today the Literary Circle is going to have an official meeting in honor of the greatest man of our epoch—Comrade Stalin.

It is warm and quiet in the room. Seated at their school desks, the members of the Literary Circle are listening to the interesting presentation by Comrade Tchalukova, "Stalin in our Poetry," attentively. Slow and deliberate ring out the words of Comrade Tchalukova as the students absorb them with thirst. A number of works by our notable poets, lyrics, are presented and thoroughly analyzed. Those clearly demonstrate the love of our working people and of our youth towards the standard-bearer of Peace, beloved leader, Stalin.

The presentation is over. A minute…Two…The room is hushed…All are under the spell of the presentation. In time, some start to fidget and whisper and some even express their admiration for the presentation loudly.

Again the room is hushed. The works presented in the competition are read.

"Ah," someone is letting a sigh out. "Written as if by an accomplished writer!"

Most satisfied by all they heard, the members of the Literary Circle are leaving the room, still discussing the presentations.

January 10, 1952
Special meeting of the Literary Circle
To help the People of Korea

Today, January 10, 1952, there was a meeting of the Literary Circle in response to the national call to action to help the people of Korea.

The room is covered in silence. All are seated on their school benches and are listening with attention the literary compositions of Comrade EP and Comrade AS in honor of the heroic people of Korea.

All their words are imprinted in the minds of the members of the Literary Circle. And again, before the end, someone is exclaiming:

"Ah, how nice!"

There were statements regarding the presented compositions by the following members: AL, KL, AS, and PP, underlining some shortcomings.

Then it was decided to create a poster in connection with the action.

Also, it was announced the National Olympiad on the theme: "What should our youth dream of?"

On leaving the meeting, all were infused with high patriotic feelings to help the people of Korea.

Follow-up:

The poster related to the action of helping the people of Korea was presented on February 3, 1952. It included the essay of Comrade EP "Help the Heroic Korea!" and the story by Comrade AS "Let Us Help the People of Korea." The artistic layout was done by Comrade IG.

The following criticism of the Elected Committee was voiced: a failure to distribute the different tasks in the best way, a failure to arrange a special meeting for the purpose of discussing the available materials and to demand the taking of responsibility for that from everybody. It was emphasized that the poster was created thanks to the perseverance of Comrade Tchalukova. In spite of that criticism, it was noted that the poster was artistically and ideologically correct.

§

Follow-up:

Comrade EP took part in the Olympiad "What should our youth dream of" with the story "Road." The story was awarded third place.

March 1, 1952
Regular meeting of the Literary Circle
Plan of activities to be discussed

1. Presentation of a paper on the theme "*The Young Guard* and the participation of the youth in the struggle against fascism reflected in the work"...AL
2. Questions and opinions/criticism regarding the paper
   a. Comrade RG made some incomplete comments regarding the format.

b. Comrade EP emphasized one of the fundamental short-comings of the paper: the lack of analyses of the variety of facts and events as well as the characters.

c. Comrade AA commented on behalf of his comrades—members of the Literary Circle of XI class. He pointed out a conflict between the good/efficient beginning/introduction of the paper and its deficient and inferior end/conclusion.

d. The comment of Comrade Tchalukova: AL succeeded only in part with the treatment of the wonderful theme the paper was on. The analysis of the events and their political essence was done without giving a thorough analysis of the characters: in spite of the commonalities, each has a particular uniqueness. She does not make a comparison between the wonderful characters of the Komsomoltsi[4] against the traitors, thus failing to demonstrate the essence of the Soviet Man. There are no facts presented for Fadeev, neither for the epoch nor his creative development. Recommendation to the rest of the members of the Literary Circle: dig deeper.

Comrade Tchalukova pointed out some positive features in the paper: first, it makes a good impression by the fact that while describing the events she shows her personal attitude toward those; secondary, the way she presented the events demonstrates another accomplishment: the novel had an influence on her.

---

4 Komsomoltsi—members of the final stage of two youth organizations with members up to age 28, graduated at 14 from the Pioneers

April 23, 1952
A celebratory meeting of the Literary Circle dedicated to First of May

Comrade E. P. opened the meeting with a short speech about the significance of one of the most cherished holidays of the working people all over the world—May First. Following that, Comrade Tchalukova recited the beautiful poem by Salis Tandjer (Салис Танджер) "Chicago—May 1, 1888."

Comrade AS read his new feuilleton "Alarm in London." It depicts the state of "Americanised" London, London of the American way of life, of banditry and debauchery. Concurrently, it pointed to the fear of the governing circles caused by the ever-increasing movement for peace while touching on the "quality" of the American manufacturing goods for export to the subservient countries. In their comments the comrades, members of the Literary Circle and guests from grade XI underlined the following mistakes:

a. Comrade EP emphasized the good beginning/introduction of the feuilleton—the depiction of the "Americanisation" of London is conveyed lively, truthfully, and engagingly. However, there was no need to introduce at the end Arsene Lupin[5]—he is not the exclusive embodiment of banditry. It would have been better to have introduced one of the bandit gangs of fanatic youth that are not a rarity in London.

b. Comrade AL remarked about the humor. Lively and juicy at the beginning, it is exceeding at the end and diminishes the artistic value of the feuilleton.

---

5 Arsene Lupin—a fictional gentleman thief and master of disguise created by French writer Maurice Leblanc.

c. Comrade Tchalukova underlined the good premise of the feuilleton, which, however, develops in the wrong direction. The effects are unsuitable, tasteless. Comrade AS should have selected other, lively, convincing ways to convey his attitude toward the Americanised England, to point out the strength and scope of the movement for peace.

Comrade EP read her new short story dedicated to the life of the Pioneers[6] entitled "Word of Honor." It deals with the attitude of the young Pioneers' detachment toward a Pioneer who received a low grade in algebra.

Comrade AA (XI B class) pointed out a certain lack of logic in the story. This lack of logic is reflected in unsuitable, empty psychological effects. This illogicality leads to unrealistic situations like the state of Boris, the shunning he is subjected to by his friends. The "Flying" meeting makes sense but is not used properly, and it does not lead to any lesson or positive outcome. The dialog is insufficient, too brief, and inferior. This diminishes the artistic quality of the short story.

Comrade DF (XIB class) concurred with the critique of his comrade. Notwithstanding the mentioned mistakes, he stated, the short story could have been a valuable contribution to our children's literature because of the obvious familiarity and understanding of the life of a Pioneer. But there should be works about more and unique heroes that include the description of more realistic acts and lively, convincing dialogs, and not empty effects. For example, Borkata could have reflected on his behavior and reached the right path before he fell asleep. But

---

6 pioneers—members of an organization for children operated by a communist party. Typically children enter into the organization in elementary school and continue until adolescence.

above all, actions are imperative. And the fundamental mistake in our comrade's literary work so far is the lack of action.

§

Follow-up:

An excursion to the village of Simeonovo was organized. Spent a very pleasant day. The lovely weather was invigorating; the cool water was refreshing, and the downpour of rain, which caught up with us in the open country, cheered us up. Got back wet but in a wonderful, fresh mood and craving for sleep.

May 16, 1952
The Visit by Comrade Zlatka Cholakova

Today we had a guest to our Literary Circle meeting, Comrade Zlatka Cholakova. She was interested in the work of our young literary cadre, so she heard some of our literary creations.

AS read his new feuilleton "Bulgaria Is not America." The following opinions were expressed in the discussion of his work: He keeps moving in this direction with ever-increasing determination, armed with uncompromising contempt for the enemies of the people and belief in the bright future of the motherland. And this feuilleton indeed is a new unquestionable achievement. With a matchless sense of humor, he depicts the attitudes of the pro-American Bulgarian bourgeoisie during the so-called reform. Comrade Zlatka Cholakova made a very poignant comment: "The reactionary force is not so naïve as you have presented it," she said. "It is treacherous and cunning. From 'The Voice of America'[7] they had learned

---

7 The broadcasts of "The Voice of America" (the official external broadcast institution of the federal government of the United States) were jammed during the

about the financial reform[8] much earlier than the workers of the country did. But they did not know the scope of its reach. This is what you should have explained, made clear, in your feuilleton."

RG read two of her poems: "Stalin" and "Dimitrov," and DF read some of his literary works.

EP read her edited short story "Let Us Help the People of Korea" as she pointed out the fundamental story line and how she used the critique as a guide in revising the story.

Plan of activities for the Literary Circle for the school year of 1952–1953
Discussions

1. "What and How to Read?"..................Comrade Tchalukova
2. "*Ivan Ivanovich*" by Antonina Koptaeva.......................AR
3. "Banners over the Towers" by Anton Semyonovich Makarenko...BK
4. "Harvester" by Yordan Yovkov..................................ET
5. "Tyutuyn" by Dimitar Dimov..................................EP
6. "Our Contemporary Poetry"...............................RG
7. "*Chovek—tova zvuchi gordo*"[9].......................(to be decided)
8. "Gorky, the Storm Bearer of the Revolution"....(to be decided)
9. "All-Conquering Power of the Works of Gorky"...(to be decided)

---

cold war years, and in particular the practice continued in Bulgaria throughout the 1970s. Listening to the broadcasts was considered an act of treason against the state.

8 Reference to the monetary reform that took place on May 10, 1952 (with coefficient of denomination 100:4).

9 *Chovek—tova zvuchi gordo* (Bulg.)—*"Man—it sounds proud"* (a popular quote from *The Lower Depths* by Maxim Gorky).

Radka Yakimov

September 15, 1952
Regular meeting of the Literary Circle

Today, January 15, 1952, took place the first get-together for the current year of the Literary Circle. The president, Comrade EP, discussed the activities of the Literary Circle during the previous school year. Mistakes made during the period were noted and a pledge was taken to avoid repeating them.

Suggestions for the future activity were presented by Comrade AS. Comrade AS recommended that the Literary Circle should create a literary magazine for the purpose of featuring the works of the members of the Literary Circle, to be selected by an editorial committee, and to organize a meeting with a cultural worker. He proposed the Literary Circle to be named "M. Gorky." The proposal was accepted unanimously by all members.

Comrade Tchalukova made a suggestion that the following initiatives be added to the agenda of the Literary Circle: to organize a trip to Koprivshtitsa-Sopot; to organize a reading conference. A decision was taken to have works by the members of the Literary Circle be read at the regular meetings. The proposal by Comrade Tchalukova regarding the name of the literary magazine was accepted as *Youth Forward*.

The old ruling committee of the Literary Circle was replaced by a new one:

1. President: Comrade EP
2. Secretary: Comrade KM

October 4, 1952
Regular meeting of the Literary Circle

Comrade Tchalukova delivered a paper on the theme "My work on the subject of *the book*." All were following the reading with great interest that was concerning a topic exciting to most of us. The essence of *the book* was coming to light in front of us: the window to the past, present, and the future; the enormous role that *the book* has played and is playing in educating us and shaping the individual.

Comrade Tchalukova pointed out how to select literary readings that will be of benefit to us: "To read a good book means to follow the thoughts of a great man" quote by Pushkin. Comrade Tchalukova recommended that all of us keep a reader's diary.

Comrade EP commented on the paper. She said that the paper touches on questions that interest her. One of her queries was how to manage our literary diary.

Comrade RG asked the question, "Should we read crime stories?" Comrade Tchalukova answered that we should read these only if we are not influenced by them, and that there is no sense in reading books of the genre because they have no literary value.

October 18, 1952
Regular meeting of the Literary Circle
Works by members of the Literary Circle to be discussed

1. "Evening Incident" and "How Charlie Holder Became a Millionaire"....TT
2. "Tito's Paradise," "The Agronomist," "Travel Notes"..........AS
3. "My Friend Masha"...EP

AS commented on the works by TT regarding their composition, style, and humor. Comrade EP stated that she did not like some of the techniques used in the short story "How Charlie Holder Became a Millionaire," and made a comment on the other short story noting that the tempo of the development of the storyline was too slow.

Comrade Tchalukova pointed out the positive sides of the first short story as well as some of its weaknesses; about the second short story, she characterized it as being incredible and unrealistic.

Comrade AS read three of his works, which we all liked. Comrade EP made a comment about his short story "Tito's Paradise" that the depiction is exaggerated. Comrade VX stated that she likes "Travel Notes," while pointing out some passages that she did not like.

In conclusion, EP read "My Friend Masha," an excerpt from her novel *Room 8*.

Comrade Tchalukova pointed out the positive aspects of the excerpt and followed with an analysis of EP's entire literary work.

December 27, 1952
Workshop meeting
Works to be discussed

1. "The Old Man Nikodim," "The Broom," "To Bankya"........TT
2. "Memories from Koprivshtitsa," "The Meeting," "Night in the Vegetable Garden"...........AS
3. *Room 8*, novel (introduction)...............................EP

Today Comrade TT read his new short story "The Old Man Nikodim." Commentary regarding the work was made by AS. He remarked that the influence of M. Gorky in the work is obvious, although there are mistakes in the use of the language, and this should be avoided. Comrade EP remarked that the old man's character is authentic. Comrade Tchalukova commented on the positive aspects of the work: It is good that TT is inspired by the romantic works of Gorky, but he should strive to create a unique one of his own. It was noted that "The Meeting" is a satirical short story. In the depiction of the morality of the bourgeoisie society in bright colors, TT is succeeding in his goal indeed. Comrade Tchalukova commented on the third short story by AS, describing it as ideologically truthful but having an unrealistic ending.

Comrade AS read his short story "Memories from Koprivshtitsa." Comrade TT commented on the work. He liked the story; the narrative is smooth, vivid in spite of the lack of dialog. Comrade EP liked the romanticism in the story regardless of some unrealistic details. The reader can't understand the uniqueness of the place; he has to convey not only the mood but also project a picture of Koprivshtitsa itself. Comrade Tchalukova recommended that AS should read the classics that have created a wonderful travelogue, to learn from them.

At the meeting was present Comrade Tomalevski, who delivered a valuable criticism of the literary works of our comrades and spoke about literature in general.

February 15, 1953
Workshop meeting

Today the opening of our Literary Circle meeting was by Comrade EP. First AS read his short story "The German." Comments were made by EP, VX, and Comrade Tchalukova. Next, AS read his feuilleton "Inspiration." Comments were made by Comrade AL regarding the humor of the work. Comrade Tchalukova pointed out some weaknesses of the work. MF said that the feuilleton does not have any of the necessary characteristics of the literary genre. It lacks focus; the names are not well chosen. It is impossible to learn any moral lessons from it; the main character should be speaking in the third person. The character of Nebenodushkov is not developed in the right light. The American reality is not exposed clearly enough. The humor in the short story is annoying and unnecessarily cynical.

Comrade EP read her short story "The Telegram." Comments were made by Comrade Tchalukova. In her opinion the subject is unsuitable; the narrative is lacking luster. EP's command of the language was not enough to save the jumble. AS made a comment regarding the style. In his opinion, the time of when the story occurs should not be of any interest.

§

The End of Stalin and the Literary Circle of Class VIIIA and VIIIB

"On March 5, 1953, at 9:50 in the evening, Comrade Joseph Vissarionovich Stalin passed away." This was the official announcement of the death of Stalin made public on the morning of the day after in Sofia. I heard it on the way during my weekly pilgrimage to the public bath in our neighborhood, blasted from the loudspeakers mounted on the building. The unconfirmed rumors had been going around for days already. Still, the statement came as a shock to me, and by the reactions of the pedestrians walking along the sidewalk at the time, it looked like all were caught by surprise. For a moment, I halted, frozen to the spot in stunned confusion, only to turn around and trot back home before the skies fell down on my head and everybody else's. The suitcase, filled with a fresh change of underwear, soap, bath towel, and the rest of the grooming paraphernalia, kept swinging from my hand, bouncing back off the calf of my leg.

It was the beginning of the end of the era later dubbed as *the period of the cult of Stalin's personality*. It was a monumental event in the historical term, but at the time, it had no immediate effect on the daily lives of ordinary people, adults and students, in one of the so-called satellite countries of the great Soviet Union. The classes of political education continued to be part of our high school curriculum, and as far as the big picture was concerned, the ideology was secure in its vastly increased domain of rule after World War II and spreading its influence abroad—fast, far and wide.

However, based on the fact that there were no more entries in the journal of the Literary Circle of VIIIA and VIIIB class beyond February 5, 1953, I feel justified in proclaiming that our Literary Circle died with Comrade Stalin's demise.

And what a fine way to go it was.

Part Two

The Fortune-Teller

The other day, Nedah had gone to a fortune-teller in the Gipsy District on the western outskirts of the city. It was not something she had intended or desired to do beforehand. She just went along accompanying her friend Vera, who had made the appointment far in advance, for Aysheh, the fortune-teller, was in high demand. Today the weather was sunny and pleasant, but the day of the meeting with Aysheh had been dark and gloomy, with fine and persistent drizzle coming down from the gray skies. All day long. It had been also a sad day, for early in the morning Nedah's mother had returned from her parents' house, where she had spent the night keeping vigil over her comatose father. She had come back home just to change her clothes and pick up some things her mother had asked for. Nedah's mother's face was pale and her eyes were swollen. So Nedah figured it out—Grandpa had passed away. Finally. He had been bedridden for a long time, and the doctors had given up on him. The inevitable had happened. Grandfather was old and had been sickly for a long time, and so it was expected. It was sad, but it was not tragic, she felt. This is why she did not cancel her engagement with Vera to accompany her on her visit to the Gipsy District. In fact, she had almost forgotten about her grandfather's passing away only a few hours earlier and was stricken with surprise—dumbfounded as a matter of fact—when Aysheh, the fortune-teller, turned her gaze toward her and said: "The soul of someone close to you departed today." It was not a question, but a statement. Nedah felt the blood drain from her face, and she could not take her eyes from Aysheh. By then, the latter had already turned her back on her and was focusing her full attention on Vera, who, at the moment, was eagerly following the fortune-teller, who was heading to the back of the tent. There, Aysheh deposited herself on the floor, cross-legged, motioned to the woman with a face brimming with tension to take a seat on a low stool, and indicated to her to stretch her arms. Next, Aysheh pulled both of Vera's hands, turned their palms up, bent her head low, and concentrated. Almost in a state of trance, she proceeded to examine each palm by touch—caressing and probing its surface as though cajoling secrets out from the lines crisscrossing the soft skin. All the while Nedah stood inside, at the very entrance of the *katun*,[10] mesmerized by the place and by Aysheh.

The tent was large and furnished rather opulently. It reminded her of the cave of Ali Baba from a movie she remembered vaguely. The entire floor was covered with thick, colorful rugs. More colorful woven rugs were hanging on the walls, and numerous pillows covered in bright, shiny, silky material were thrown all over the floor. A brass vase was placed on a low round table. Aysheh's attire was just as striking and colorful, although it was not as unusual as the decor of the tent's interior, for many of the women of this district wore the same *shalvars*[11] and kerchiefs as the one covering the dark hair of the fortune-teller. The shiny deep-blue silk was pulled tightly over her forehead and all the way around the top of her head; its ends were hanging from a tight knot, spilling over her shoulders. Nedah had lost track of the time when Aysheh stood up, nimbly and gracefully, indicating the end of the séance. Nedah's friend stood up from her chair, reluctantly and slowly, opened up her handbag, pulled something from its inside, and placed it

10 *katun*—Roma's (Gipsy's) traditional tent.

11 *shalvars*—items of Roma (Gipsy) women's traditional attire.

into Aysheh's hand. Swiftly the latter shoved it in the high décolleté of her blouse. Then, Aysheh turned around and headed toward the exit and the woman standing by. The fortune-teller's eyes, fixed on Nedah's face, penetrated hers with magnetic power.

"Is there something you want to ask me about?" she said in a low voice, portentous of hidden messages and deep secret knowledge.

"How did you know about the departed soul?" Nedah asked.

"I also know that you love a man, but you don't trust him," the fortune-teller said, continuing to skirt the question.

Nedah kept silent.

"Your star is weak," Aysheh continued, in a tone of voice that sounded cold and impartial, yet Nedah felt that there was a hint of disdain in it. So she stubbornly kept quiet.

"If you give me fifty leva[12] I will ask the mufti in the mosque to say a prayer for you," Aysheh said, and, without waiting further for a response, she turned around and retreated toward the back of the tent.

Meanwhile, Vera had moved toward the exit and was standing next to Nedah, occasionally dabbing her eyes with a handkerchief and drying up the moisture of tears from her cheeks.

"Let's go," Nedah said—rather, commanded—while grabbing her friend by the sleeve of her coat.

Outside the tent, standing at the edge of the sidewalk covered in loose concrete tiles wet from the fine, relentless rain, were the empty streets of the enclave, comprised of a variety of ramshackle, low-to-the-ground structures lining meandering streets covered in stone bricks. The two women were walking brusquely—eyes lowered, watching their steps, squeezed tightly under a large black umbrella, which Nedah held firmly in her hand. The rhythmic clatter of a horse's hooves beating

---

12 leva (levs)—plural of *lev*, the Bulgarian monetary unit.

the stone pavement and the sound of wooden wheels running over the hard road surface was growing in intensity. Presently, a perky horse with a shiny brown coat and a large red pompon mounted over and between his eyes—cheerfully swinging in all directions in unison with the horse's stride—passed them, pulling a cart full of junk. An elderly man in unremarkable attire with a swarthy face sat on the seat of the cart, holding a whip that he lashed rather ceremoniously in the air, a gesture strictly meant to reassure the two pedestrian women walking along the sidewalk that he was in control of the animal. After a few turns in the maze of nondescript streets, they came to Stambolijski Boulevard and headed in an easterly direction toward the Sveta Nedelya Church designating the end of the street, visible far in the distance. At one point Nedah had snapped at her friend, "Watch your steps!" as she had stumbled in a pothole created by a missing tile in the sidewalk. "It is going to be all right…" she had mumbled as she tightened the hold on her friend's forearm. The rest of the way passed in silence.

Inside Café Levski, on the southeast corner of Rakovska Street and Aksakov Street, Nedah and her friend sat, sipping linden tea with lemon. The front of Nedah's gray coat was left wide open. It was the month of October, but felt almost like spring.

"Sorry about your grandfather's passing away," Vera said. Her expressive, almond-shaped eyes shone with a warm glow. "Thanks for accompanying me to the fortune-teller's place." After a short pause she added, "Didn't feel like going alone in the district…you know…"

"Never mind," Nedah murmured as she placed the cup of tea back on the table after taking a small sip. "It was interesting…Never been to a fortune-teller before." As soon as she heard the last syllable pass her lips, she regretted her lack of tact. Her friend was staring past her, with eyes that had turned bright and luminous from moisture suddenly rushing to them.

"Did you hear what Aysheh said to me as we entered the *katun*?" Nedah said in a hurried manner. "It was extraordinary," she nearly shouted. "How did she know that my grandfather had died this same day?"

Nedah was leaning over the table, her rising voice and her intense stare betraying eagerness that startled her friend.

"Did she say that, really?" Vera's face had transformed—glowing, overcome by a hopeful feeling. "Oh, I didn't hear her. I was feeling so—" She checked herself and stopped, falling into an embarrassed silence.

"Are you wearing a black ribbon on your coat?" Vera asked suddenly.

"No, I'm not. There was no way she could have known simply by looking at me," Nedah said with excitement. "I was shocked to hear her say that!"

"She is good. Really good…"

"Should have given her the fifty levs," Nedah said quietly.

"What are you talking about?" Vera asked with a frown.

"Never mind…" Nedah murmured.

The House on the Corner

The four-story house located at the intersection of a wide street running in an east–west direction and a cozy, short, and narrower street running in the north–south direction was in an advanced state of disrepair, like the rest of the buildings in the area, which were predominantly low apartments or two-story houses. The only distinction of this structure from an architectural point of view was its height, which caused some consternation in those trying to describe the type of dwelling it was to a person not acquainted with the place. By the look of it, it was a house, but by its size and capacity as a housing unit, it was more akin to an apartment building. At least this was the impression created in most of the young people unaccustomed to a family dwelling of that size and the number of inhabitants residing in it now. Those were some of the thoughts going through Nedah's mind in the late afternoon on this particular day as she threaded along the wide sidewalk of the wide street on her way back home from work. The sun was setting behind her back, and the view ahead of her, of the house on the corner, was crisp and pretty in the clear air. She could hear the sound of music drifting from the few open windows of the apartment buildings overlooking the street: the screeching sound of a violin, the uneven rhythm of a musical phrase practiced on a piano. Those were the sounds that she loved, for they brought a sense of serenity and peace in her, of order and permanence. The only traffic on the street—if it could be categorized in this way—consisted of a few kids on bicycles, passing her with their hands off the handles and legs stretched away from the pedals as they coasted along the street, propelled by the inertia of the downhill incline.

Just opposite from the house on the corner stood a small store; the doors were closed and secured by padlocks. Outside the store, a few bicycles leaned against the wall of the building. An old sign on top read: "Bicycles for rent." *How sad,* Nedah thought as she glanced at the sign, the bicycles, and the rusty padlocks—all covered in grime. The store has been closed for years and left to neglect, along with half a dozen other private small enterprises in the neighborhood. The only ones in operation were a couple of the government-owned grocery stores with empty shelves inside and queues outside seen at different and unpredictable times of the day. From the corner of her eye, Nedah could see one of those lines stretching along the sidewalk in front of the grocery store at the corner, a block away up the street.

Presently, she turned right, entering the backyard through the left-open iron gate, and proceeded along the pathway running next to the wall of the west side of the house leading to the side entrance of the dwelling. Just before reaching the wooden double door, also left wide open, she smiled while inhaling the aroma of a slowly simmering dish made of fresh vegetables and plenty of seasonings drifting from the open window of the suite on the parterre[13] floor. Sun rays streaming through the window on the landing facing west lit up the narrow stairway leading to the upper floors. The old dark-brown steps, made of solid oak, emitted squeaking noises under Nedah's feet as she climbed all the way up to the third floor, where she shared a couple of high-ceilinged, spacious rooms with her parents. The first thing that she saw as she entered was a slight middle-aged man who slumbered in an armchair; his eyes

---

13 Parterre (Fr.)—the first floor of a multistory building, on a level about a meter higher than street level.

were closed, and a soft and monotonous vibrating sound came from his nostrils in synchrony with the shallow movement of his chest. Careful not to disturb the man in his chair, Nedah proceeded to the adjacent room, where she took off her high-heeled, pointed-toe shoes and placed them on the bottom shelf of the huge wardrobe, then pulled a pair of slippers from under one of the beds and shoved her feet into them. She took off her raincoat and hung it on the stand in one of the room's corners. Then she strode back past the still-sleeping man and exited the room. She crossed the landing and passed through the first door to the right, which led into the communal kitchen. The door to the left led to the washroom shared by the people living on the same floor in the rest of the rooms. The kitchen was empty, but Nedah knew that this was not to last for long, as dinnertime was only a couple of hours away, and the time for preparation of the food was already at hand.

The days were getting shorter, and the light streaming into the east-facing room was fading slowly. The colorful oilcloth covering the top of the kitchen table was covered in crumbs, and a couple of dirty dishes were piled and left there, with hardened food and spoons left inside them. A couple of stained glasses soaked in the kitchen sink. Someone must have left in a hurry after lunch. The pattern on the dishes was familiar, and Nedah did not waste time contemplating what to do. Quickly, she cleared the table and placed the dirty dishes in the sink, wiped the top of the tablecloth with a piece of rag she kept in the drawer designated for her family's use, and got busy with preparing the evening meal of mishmash.

A few hours later, Nedah was striding along the street, in a westerly direction, on her way to a destination farther southwest from her house, heading to an apartment building located in a district away from the closest public transportation. And because she did not like traveling with buses and streetcars full of tightly packed crowds, this was just fine. The cast-down eyes, the rhythm of her marching steps, the hands pushed deep in her pockets, and the manner in which her arm was squeezing the handbag hanging from her shoulder all pointed to the tension and absentmindedness of her mood. For weeks she had felt the pressure at home, coming from her mother in not-too-subtle ways, and at work, exerted by her friend and coworker in ways not more delicate than those of her mother. The matter concerned her friend's brother. Or, more precisely, it was about getting the coveted status of Sofia citizenship. The law required that one's citizenship was determined by the place of one's birth, but, as in all aspects of life, there were exceptions, or, more precisely put, there were ways to circumvent the predicament. Nothing new under the sky…

And there were the incentives.

For the militiamen (the policemen from the past) and those willing to work in the newly constructed "Kremikovtsi"—a sprawling industrial complex for the production of cast iron, steel, and other metals—there were opportunities and hard choices to be made. The vast compound, located on the eastern outskirts of the capital city of Sofia, its chimneys sticking high in the sky, blowing yellow smoke drifting in all directions, spread its foul-smelling blanket of pollution far and wide.

For the educated, more sophisticated, unlucky provincials, the easiest or preferred way was by marriage to a citizen of Sofia. In this case, though, one had to be very careful, for a spinster born in Sofia could stick to her guns and refuse to go through with the divorce the other party was counting on when getting into this arrangement.

And this was the case with Nedah's coworker and her brother. Both were born in a small town a couple of hundred kilometers away from Sofia, and therefore were not entitled by birthright to Sofia citizenship. So they had to find ways to overcome the consequences of the misfortunate fact of having been brought into this world in a place not entirely to their tastes, a condition usually discovered on reaching maturity. After spending six years away from his native town, the coworker's brother had to leave the capital city and go back "home." The time for action had arrived. Years earlier, Nedah's friend and coworker had resolved the problem successfully for herself and now was pursuing the same strategy for her brother's benefit.

In all fairness, it should be said that not everyone was dreaming of a life as the ultimate urbanite in a small Balkan country, but those young people who found themselves in this young man's situation, once bitten by the bug, felt doomed—a feeling very much akin to the one experienced by an unlucky soul who has just received an undeserved prison sentence. Not that the capital city was a bustling, lively, and charming place like the ones they had seen on the pages of smuggled Western magazines, but there were streetcars, movie houses, and a degree of privacy—the possibility of creating an illusion of personal freedom. A stubborn idea some found hard to let fade away...

Nedah stood in front of the solid wooden door with a shiny brass plate attached right under the peeping hole—bearing the etched inscription of *D-r Marinov*—awkwardly moving her gaze away from the small round contraption in front of her, conscious of the scrutiny of the eye stuck to the magnifying glass on the inside of the apartment, taking measure of her. A faint smile crossed her face as the figure of a plump middle-aged woman appeared in the frame of the open door and motioned her to enter the foyer. Behind the woman, the silhouette of a tall man with his back turned to the windows stood at attention. Nedah felt her lips tighten.

"Meet my brother Peppy," the plump lady said, pointing to the tall man at her side.

"Petar," he blurted, stretching his arm to Nedah for a handshake.

The plump lady scurried in the direction of the kitchen, leaving the two young people staring at each other. A quick glance at his freshly ironed white shirt, the crease of his pants, and the slippers on his feet—favored by pensioners—increased her discomfort at the thought of how much effort her friend had put into preparing her brother for this meeting. The feeling was mixed with resentment caused by a sneaking suspicion that the young man lacked as much enthusiasm as she did and felt uncomfortable with the scheme just as strongly as she did. The thought irked her.

Twilight was descending fast over the city, and the streets were filling up with pedestrians in a hurry to do some chores, or just leaving work and heading home at the end of the working hours. Meanwhile, in front of the row of telephone booths in Slaveikov Square—lined up in front of the building of Alliance Francais and the movie house—the familiar scene of people standing, waiting for their dates to show up, in a variety of poses exuding anxious anticipation, had assembled. Nedah entered one of the empty booths, took the phone from the hook, and concentrated on dialing the six digits of the telephone number imprinted in her memories for years, patiently waiting while listening to the metallic hum of the dial plate on its counterclockwise rotation back to the zero position after each figure. The ring following a short silence indicated a free line, and in few moments a pleasant woman's voice inquired, "Hello. Who is calling?" And then she said, "Sorry, Nedah, he isn't at home."

The pedestrian traffic along the drag on Rakovska Street, or Raksy, as it was referred to by the younger generation, had swelled in the last half an hour from a trickle of leisurely strolling small groups of two or three to a stream of excited crowds spilling from the sidewalks into the road, trotting over to the other side to greet acquaintances or friends moving in the opposite direction. And for some inexplicable reason, the movement along the drag followed rules similar to those of a motor traffic, although not necessarily in a permanent fashion. The flow in the southern direction usually stuck to the eastern side of the street, while the flow in the northern direction often ran along the western side of the road. As Nedah strode on the west sidewalk, her eyes scoured the interiors of the cafés and restaurants as she passed by. As she passed Restaurant Ashinger, she recognized the face of the famous opera singer Ilka Popova, seated at a table next to the window opposite her much younger husband. As usual, her face resembled a frozen mask, quite the opposite of the image on a portrait of hers displayed in the window of a haberdashery store on the other side of the street—her face beautifully radiant, her hair covered in an elaborate tiara in the role of the feisty Carmen for a production in the Paris Opera House of long ago. At the corner of Café Levsky, Nedah took a sharp turn to the right and continued along Aksakov Street. The streetlights had been turned on, and the garden in front of the Military Club to the left was empty, except for an odd man or woman taking the shortcut to Boulevard Ruski—avoiding the hubbub of the drag—and the shadows of lovers embracing, lost in worlds of their own. *Fifty leva and I could be one of those,* Nedah thought, glancing in the direction of the garden. She tried to chase away the nagging thought by drowning all her senses in the noise of sparrows' wings flapping in the air and the rustle beneath her feet of the fallen leaves that surrounded her.

The tempo of her strides kept slowing, until by the time she reached the end of Aksakov Street, crossed Tolbuhin Street, and reached the corner of the small park, she hardly could drag her feet any farther. Not far from the light post and close to an arch made of stone, for a purpose that was not at all clear, was an empty bench. It was a peaceful and secluded place. Yet safe. Nedah dropped on the middle of the wooden bench. Just like that...

A couple of hours later she got back home. Her mother was waiting and eager.

"How did it go?" she asked as soon as she saw her daughter enter the room.

"Fine. Just fine…" Nedah whispered. "Leave me alone, Mom. He is a good-looking fellow. He would find someone else…" she added. For a while, there was nothing but silence, heavy with the unspoken words of a conversation that had been going on for far too long and that, by now, had brought nothing but exhaustion in both mother and daughter.

"I must be worth more than a Sofia citizenship," were the only words spoken by Nedah, who had already gone to bed and curled up under the padded duvet made of gold brocade. Her voice came low and muffled by the pillow. Her mother's sigh came loud and clear.

Nedah's friend, Vera, was also her neighbor, one of the many inhabitants of the house on the corner, sharing bathrooms and kitchens fashioned from rooms that had been designed and built to serve an entirely different purpose, converted just to meet immediate needs and without any considerations for practicality. Vera's family of four, including Vera's younger brother Michael, or Misho, as he was called by relatives and friends, occupied the parterre floor of the house. And that had its advantages and disadvantages. The most important of the first was that because the total area of the floor space was reduced by a unit, on account of the space taken by the entrance foyer, their place ended up with a private kitchen, but they had to share the washroom with the occupants of the upper floors. And because all of the residents were renters of property owned by city hall, no one had the inclination (or the means) to do anything about it. Just a potty would do.

Vera was a few years older than Nedah and still unmarried. It was not that she did not want to marry, but rather that the man she wanted was not available. Or unwilling. Or simply not ready to enter matrimony and get tied to a woman like Vera. He procrastinated. It was harder and harder for Vera to listen to her mother's lamentations, to look at her father and see the unhappiness in his eyes and feel guilty about her inability to break away from the prison of her unrequited love. Somewhere, sometime before, she had heard about the fortune-teller Aysheh. And the other day she had gone to her looking for a miracle. She had asked Nedah to accompany her not because she felt very close to her, but rather because she was not a close friend, just a neighbor who did not poke her nose into other people's business. And that was what she needed right now.

On that day, when she had gone to Aysheh and spent an hour in small talk with Nedah in Café Levsky, she returned home in a better frame of mind than she had experienced for a while. The smile she wore on her face as she greeted her parents only elicited looks of bewilderment and slight irritation from both. Her mother dropped her knitting in her lap, and her father turned a page of the large newspaper he was reading as he readjusted his position in the old armchair upholstered in worn-out brocade—its color and the pattern of the design woven into the fabric appearing as nothing more than a vague suggestion.

"You seem cheerful," her mother said.

"Went to the cinema. Saw a French movie with Fernandell," Vera said without a pause. "All week long they are going to show French movies in the cinemas…" The words trailed as she disappeared behind the kitchen door. Once inside, she leaned against the wall right next to the doorframe, pushing at the hard surface with her entire body, overwhelmed by fatigue, too weak to lift an arm and wipe the tears trickling down her cheeks. Lies… lies…easy to come on command, but still hard on her consciousness.

§

Darkness was descending fast over the city in the grip of late-December melancholy. With her head bowed and her eyes concentrated on each cement tile covering the sidewalk, Nedah made her way home at the end of her working day. The raised collar of her gray coat provided some protection against the sharp chill. The high heels of her stiletto shoes, stripped of their leather, kept sinking in the cracks and grooves in and between the broken tiles. The thought of approaching winter, with the inevitable snow and slush, had hit her suddenly and brought regrets for spending half a month's salary to acquire the fashionable shoes (made in Greece!) from the black market. *Will have to make it somehow through the winter,* she thought. By the time she reached the house on the corner and climbed the three flights of stairs, her mood had reached a low point.

Her mother appeared from the communal kitchen, quickly crossed the landing, and pushed her inside the room of their unit.

"Vera was taken to the hospital," she whispered. "Swallowed a hundred pills. Chloroquine…"

Nedah pulled out a chair, following the example of her mother, who already had settled herself in an armchair and was leaning forward, staring at her daughter with a poignant intensity that had more to do with her concern for her own child than for the desperate person she was referring to. Then she started relaying the story in a whisper, fast and careful, listening for any sound coming from behind the door, waiting for the slightest noise to fade away, making sure no one would hear her tale except her daughter, Nedah. Hiding by reflex—a second nature by now.

The day before yesterday, around midmorning, Nedah's mother was washing a few mugs and the frying pan left in the kitchen sink from the last night's meal when she felt a silent presence behind her back. Someone was waiting to use the sink, she assumed, and she felt irked. The people they shared the facilities with should have left for work a couple of hours ago. So she was sure that she would have the kitchen for herself. A gentle touch on her shoulder startled her.

"Good morning, Mrs. Gueorgieva. Would you, please, do me a favor?" Vera said as Nedah's mother turned around and faced her.

"Of course, Vera," Mrs. Gueorgieva said. "But of course!" she emphasized. "What can I do for you?" she asked eagerly. Her irritation had turned into alarm. The woman in front of her was pale; her eyes radiated sadness so profound and hard to grasp at the spur of the moment—matched only by the fragility emanating from her entire body.

"Are you ill?"

"Can you lend me some money, Mrs. Gueorgieva? Need to buy something...urgently," she blurted. "Ran out of money before the advance,[14] which is coming in a couple of days," she added assuredly.

It was not an unusual request, and Mrs. Gueorgieva did not hesitate before saying yes.

"What is the amount you need?" she asked.

"Twenty leva," Vera said. Mrs. Gueorgieva waved her to follow her inside their quarters. A few moments later, tightly squeezing the banknotes in her fist, Vera headed to the door. A few steps away from the threshold, she stopped.

"Please, do not mention this to my parents. Let it stay a matter strictly between us both," she said in a low voice, then opened the door and quickly disappeared behind it. And this was the last time Mrs. Gueorgieva had seen Vera before she saw the ambulance today in front of the house.

It was late, and long after the regular visiting hours at the hospital had passed. It was possible that visiting hours were canceled entirely on account of a flu epidemic, or some other obscure reason, Nedah thought. As far as Nedah's mother knew, Vera had survived the immediate danger, and now all that mattered was the possible side effects of the medication taken in such large dose, which Nedah worried about. Also, she was not that close to Vera and felt that her visit to the hospital would not be appreciated by her friend. Instead of comfort, it could

---

14 advance—first installment of the monthly salary paid in cash. The advance was paid in the middle of the month and the rest of the sum at the end of it.

bring embarrassment. So Nedah got up from her chair and went to change in the other room. Also, she needed to be alone. Meanwhile, Mrs. Gueorgieva's thoughts seemed to have drifted away in a different direction: *I shouldn't have given her the money. Did she use it for buying the pills? What would her parents and the neighbors think if they knew I lent her the money?* She kept moaning.

The top floor of the house on the corner had been transformed from an attic with a high cathedral ceiling to a unit consisting of two bedrooms and no service rooms. The main purpose for the large and bright area as originally built was for drying the laundry of the large family occupying the large house once upon a time. At that time, a number of clotheslines ran across the entire length of the attic, and a couple of windows in the shape of semicircles installed in the roof's recesses provided enough sunlight and draft for the laundry to dry. Now all that space was transformed into a two-room unit, each created to accommodate the location of the windows. Unfortunately, the lack of plumbing precluded any possibility of partitioning part of the area for kitchen or toilet utilization. The current occupants had to share the ones on the lower floor. Mrs. Filipova installed an electric-wire hot plate and did most of her cooking and heating of water for washing the clothes and dishes in the privacy of her room—one with a great view and the advantage of having living quarters on the top of the building, with no creaking and cracking noises coming through the ceiling to disturb her at any time of day or night. Maria Filipova shared her place with her son Anton, or Tony, as he was called, a handsome young man with locks of wavy black hair hanging over half of his high brow, a quick smile, and a gait suggestive of an impatient disposition—always fidgeting, never still. The never-present Mr. Filipov was a source of constant curiosity and speculation among the rest of the inhabitants of the house on the corner.

Late in the evening, at the end of the day on which the ambulance was spotted in front of the house on the corner—a day spent in lively excitement fed by whispered gossip and speculations—the calm was disturbed by a familiar noise: Tony skipping along the wooden staircase. There was the thud of the final jump at the bottom of the last flight of stairs, and finally the quiet set in. On the top floor, Mrs. Filipova went through her nightly ritual: She put on her nightgown; dissolved a small paper bag of sleeping powder in a glass of water, which she swallowed quickly; pulled the cover off of her bed; and squeezed under the thick duvet as she exhaled a deep sigh.

§

Slowly, Vera turned her head to her left. A heavy moan was drifting from the occupant of the bed, a woman in her mid-thirties who had been brought in the day before. Next to the woman's bed, a man was sitting, looking uncomfortable, just staring at the woman's face and her closed eyes, listening to her moans. The woman slowly opened her eyes and fixed her gaze on the man. Immediately the man shifted his eyes away, meeting Vera's, only to turn them away instantly from her and back toward the woman. Hastily, he pulled up his right hand, which had been hanging limply by his side, and placed it on her crossed palms resting on the blanket. The wedding bands told the story, Vera thought, turning her head away from the scene that played to her left. A low mutter replaced the previous sound. Vera buried her head in the pillow and closed her eyes. The large room was filled with light streaming through the recently washed windows, showing the streaks left by the wet newspaper used to dry the cleaning liquid. The emptiness inside her was complete; her body felt paralyzed by fatigue.

She tried to remember. But the only images that filled the darkness in her brain were of all those beds she had shared with men she did not care for and did not even remember clearly, as the only reason she had ended up there in the first place was to forget the one man she wanted but couldn't have. It had worked for a while, for a short time, until it turned into the nightmare that she had tried to put an end to the other day. It seems that she had succeeded in one way by purging her mind of the men, but not of those beds...

A hushed "hello" woke her from the slumber she had drifted into a while ago. Vera opened her eyes. At a glance, she saw a figure standing next to her bed with a small bouquet in hand. From the corner of her eye she saw the next bed; the man was gone, and the back of her neighbor was turned toward her.

"How do you feel?" Nedah asked with a pleasant smile. She left the flowers on the side table before gingerly taking a seat at the edge of the bed.

An awkward silence followed. Vera's eyes grew large and turned bright, brimming with tears. Nedah threw herself over her and wrapped her arms around Vera's shoulders in a tight embrace.

Half an hour later, Nedah was walking along the sidewalk outside the hospital, looking for something. A block away, she entered an empty telephone booth and dialed a number written on a piece of paper that she had been squeezing in her fist along the way.

"Hello. This is Nedah, a friend of Vera's." There was silence on the other side. After a brief hesitation, she continued.

"I'd like to inform you that Vera is at the Alexandrovska Hospital... Took an overdose of chloroquine..." All she could distinguish was a tentative "hmm..." coming from the other end of the connection. She was about to hang up when she heard the male voice, the words coming out cold, smarting with annoyance.

"I have nothing to do with that," the man said.

Nedah replaced the phone back on its hook and left the booth.

The Party, the Reluctant
Collaborator, and the Mad House

The party that had started a couple of hours earlier had run halfway
through its course. The air was thick with cigarette smoke and the
pungent odor of alcohol. A few, mostly empty, bottles of wine and plum
brandy—the main providers of energy and stimulation for the high
intensity of the dancing—were left on the coffee table next to a couple
of ashtrays full of squashed cigarette butts and plates covered with hardened remnants of sandwiches and crumbs. Dirty glasses of great variety were scattered over the floor and on any flat surface available. The
dancing had been over for a while, except for the slow-moving couple
in a tight embrace, swaying over the same spot in a state of ecstasy or
oblivion—hard to distinguish one way or the other. The bright lights of
the electric fixture hanging from the ceiling inside the apartment were
switched off, and the overall mood of the gathering had morphed from
joyfully celebratory to wistfully romantic.

The pale light streaming in from the outside provided by the few
lampposts standing at the edge of the sidewalk below the windows
overlooking the street illuminated the interior of the apartment's living room, crowded with furniture and people. The music flowing from
the tape player filled the darkened room with the eclectic sounds of
American music of all genres. The sound mixed with the whisperings,
giggles, muffled female protestations, cajoling male voices, and noise

produced by cloth rubbing against cloth in the push and shove of nego-
tiating through complicated rituals of lovemaking—or rather, attempts
at it—by intertwined couples curled all over the furniture. The scene
was a familiar one repeated in different settings, the ongoing tug-of-war
between the sexes, challenging the limits set by traditional taboos and
the contemporary hypocrisy in a society under siege, bombarded with
slogans proclaiming equality and emancipation, all the while ruled by
men exclusively.

A distinct whimpering sound came from one of the corners of the
room, where a young woman was seated on a chair, her shoulders and
head drooping over her chest. Her long hair mingled with the unruly
mess of wisps of hair belonging to a guy seated on the floor, at her feet,
with his head buried in her lap. His shoulders kept shaking at intermit-
tent intervals in synchrony with the intensity of the caresses bestowed
all over his back and head by the girl's hands. The tape must have run
out, as the loud music seized abruptly and the words "Sorry! I am so
sorry..." cut through the silence in a voice laden with drama. A guy got
up and approached the table on which the tape player sat and switched
the empty roll with a full one. The music started to flow again, and the
guy returned to his sweetheart.

The party went on. Finally, it was getting late, and a couple of girls
were standing up, ready to leave, waiting for the guys to light their cigarettes before going down the staircase and into the street for the leisurely walk back home. The music had stopped a while ago and nobody
bothered to change the rolls. Another coupon[15] was coming to its end,
and nothing had changed. The same couples, the same drama, the same
escape into a fantasy world built up in the minds of young men and
women on the strength of forbidden music smuggled from paradise. The

---

15 coupon (slang)—party.

awareness of the mundane reality of their everyday lives was slowly setting back in. Tomorrow morning the hangovers would come...

And then the door burst open, and a handsome young man staggered in.

"Hi!" he said as he dropped to the floor, his back sliding against the casing of the closed door. "Sit down and pay attention! I got something important to tell you all." He shoved his hand inside his jacket, took an object out of it, and placed it on the floor in front of his crossed legs. "Here, this is the patlak[16] I have been issued by the MVR,"[17] he blurted. The young man just sat there with his eyes focused on the black metallic object on the floor in front of him, with an aura of detachment and wonderment akin to the sentiments expressed in the countenance of all present. It was a surreal scene nobody could make any sense of.

"I am supposed to spy on you and report. I have become a collaborator in exchange for dropping the charges..."

"What charges? What are you talking about? You are totally smashed, and you are losing your mind!" said a male voice, breaking the silence.

"Why would MVR be interested in us? Pick up your toy and let me take you home," another young man said, approaching the door. He froze near the object.

"This is the real thing..." he hissed.

"What did you expect?" the guy sitting on the floor hissed back. "Would I kid about such a thing, and why do you think I got smashed? Been walking around...Been thinking...For days...What should I do?" He lifted his head and stared at the guy who had offered to take him

---

16 patlak (slang)—gun.

17 MVR—Ministry of Internal Affairs. In this case, it is used in a broad sense that includes the Secret Service.

home. Tears ran down his cheeks. "So I came to tell you that you should stay away from me, and I will stay away from you..."

"How did you get into this mess?" asked the other young man. "Let's go," he said, finally, giving up hope on getting an answer to his question. Silent people started moving, filing through the door, averting their gaze from the duo by the door. Outside the building, someone was whispering to a couple of guys.

"He got nicked by the stopanska militia[18] for black marketeering. Selling rose oil." One of the guys in the group gawked in confusion. "What are you staring like that for? It is genuine rose oil I am talking about. Not the cheap rose essence sold in the stores for souvenirs. Rose oil is a government commodity and forbidden to sell."

"Wow, what a fantastic story," the guy said, his face still screwed up in disbelief. "Where does one get stuff like that?"

§

In front of the spotty mirror with cracked corners attached to the wall over the cracked, gone-dull white porcelain sink, its water tap encrusted with lime and grease, Nedah stood leaning over, covering her plump lips with layers of pink lipstick. She had just finished washing her face with a thin sliver of soap—someone had left it behind—and wiped it with her hanky.

This morning she had overslept after last night's party, and there was no time left to hang around on the landing, waiting for whoever was occupying the bathroom to get out. She had run the comb through her hair while running down the stairs and rushed to catch the streetcar for work. She had wished that she had been able at least to take her toothbrush and toothpaste so she could clean her teeth

---

18   stopanska militia (Bul.)—Trade Police.

and get rid of the unpleasant taste in her mouth left from last night's indulgence with Pliska cognac and cigarettes. Her head ached. On her walk from the tram stop to the office building, her stilettos had given her a hard time; they kept getting stuck between the cobblestones—tripping her, raising her anxieties to a new high. In the entrance hall of the building and along its left she had seen the guard, seated behind the sliding glass panels of his booth, observing the front door, scrutinizing anyone coming through with an eagle eye. Passing in a rush by the guard, Nedah had murmured "Good morning," skipped over a couple of stairs running across the floor, and entered the long corridor. Two doors to the right was a nondescript door painted in glossy white paint gone yellow around the knob. She had pushed it open and heard it slam shut behind her back. She had felt relief at the sight of the three empty desks. It was obvious that her two colleagues had already arrived, left their stuff on the top of their desks, and gone out of the office before settling down. Quickly, she had taken off her overcoat, grabbed her purse, and scurried back along the corridor. Now, the sound of the washroom door being opened and slammed shut behind her alerted her to pull herself forward in expectation of the push inevitably to come from the person entering the cramped space in front of the mirror.

"Hi."

A greeting and a shove to move a bit came from her right side. Her colleague was standing next to her with stretched hands, trying to get hold of the tap. Nedah pulled away from the sink and dropped the lipstick into the pocket slit in the side seams of her skirt.

"Hi," she said. "Got a bit of a hangover," she added.

"Hmm…It shows." Her colleague's smiling eyes were looking at her reflected image in the mirror. "Don't feel like spending an entire day behind the desk, do you?" she said as she shook the excess water from her hands before wiping them dry with a couple of pieces of newspaper cuttings she had brought from the cubicle, where they were stuck on a long nail driven into the wall.

Nedah shrugged her shoulders.

"How about taking the afternoon off?" The colleague's intense stare was fixed on Nedah's face. "I'll come by your office and pick you up after lunch."

"All right," Nedah said.

The complex of the Alexandrovska Hospital consisted of a large multi-story building facing a wide boulevard and a number of smaller structures sprawling behind it over an area obscured by the dominant façade of the main one. At least this was the impression Nedah carried in her mind up to the moment that she and her colleague entered a narrow path leading to a small building that looked like an isolated and lonely place. She felt confused, even a bit lost, as anxiety crept up inside her. Close to an hour ago they had passed by the guard's cubicle in the foyer of the Institute. The guard had stood up from his seat in a low chair inside the room, approached the window, and pulled one of the glass panels up along the frame slides.

"Where are you going, you two?" he had inquired with a smile, pushing forward a thick book, its pages spread under the glass partition over the extended ledge.

"To the Ministry," each one had murmured while signing the attendance book, then proceeded with few sharp tugs at the handles of their large purses to bring into view the conspicuously displayed folders sticking out from them. The guard had pulled the book back and slammed closed the glass firmly against the frame before dropping back into his chair with arms folded in front of his bulging chest. A wide yawn distorted his fleshy face.

A nurse dressed in a white coat opened the door and peeked to the left and then to the right along the corridor before stepping aside to let the two young women enter her office.

"Give me a minute to finish the paperwork," she said, pointing to the desk covered with loose paper sheets while walking them to an open door leading to the outside. The two women gingerly stepped down the few worn-out concrete steps leading to the backyard, which was surrounded by high walls. A distant hum coming from the direction of the outside world was audible. Still, inside the walls surrounding the area, the feeling of an eerily quiet isolation was overwhelming. About ten male patients were milling about like ghosts—self-absorbed in a world of their own. Some were muttering torrents of words under their breath—indistinguishable mumbo-jumbo of an endless monologue with unseeing eyes outside their internal, crowded universe. A pale young man with plentiful dark hair kept walking in circles with an empty, tragically melancholic stare.

"This one snapped during a performance," Nedah heard the whisper in her ear. "Very talented pianist…" the friend added in a tone of voice laden with sympathy. Suddenly a disheveled, robust middle-aged man appeared in front of the two women, his eyes flashing with pride as he presented himself in earnest as Napoleon Bonaparte.

The nurse who had just joined the duo said, "How are you doing today, Comrade Bonaparte?" The man switched his glance from Nedah to the intruder in a white coat, screwed up his face in disdain, and turned around and walked away.

"This one is a schizophrenic," the nurse said in a casual tone. "Today he is Napoleon, but tomorrow he might turn into a saint. One can never be sure…"

A man drifted from one of the yard's corners in the direction of the spot where the three women were standing, then stopped and fixed his stare on Nedah, not in a threatening way, but as if in wonderment of trying to recollect something or somebody, with inquisitive, penetrating eyes.

"What is behind this wall?" Nedah asked the nurse, averting her eyes from the man staring at her, and the discomfort it brought over her.

"The women's ward," said the nurse. "You can take a look from the landing up the stairs if you'd like to see the patients milling about in the backyard," she continued. Yes, Nedah wanted to see what was behind those high walls. So she climbed back up the stairs and onto the landing.

The first face she saw clearly was that of a short young woman, indistinguishable from the rest, slow moving, self-absorbed, dressed in loosely fitting garb of an indistinguishable shade. The eyes that looked back at Nedah were vacant, and the woman's face was blank. Presently, she turned around and leisurely shuffled off, joining the rest in their aimless wandering in the shadows of the high walls surrounding the courtyard. Quickly, Nedah turned around, scurried down the staircase, and proceeded toward the exit.

"Let's go," she blurted as she passed her companion and kept marching forward.

Outside the building, her friend inquired, "What is the matter? Why the rush?"

"Got to get back in half an hour," Nedah muttered.

§

The chimes of the grandfather clock—shoved into one of the corners of the dining room—reverberated throughout the apartment: *one, two, three, four.* The lady, in her late forties and dressed in an off-white raincoat on top of a sweater over an emprime[19] satin dress in a flower print, kept counting the melodious strokes loudly while scurrying toward the front door on her way out to a meeting of the neighborhood's Section of the United organization. Clearly she was in a foul mood, as could be judged by the annoyance in her voice with the clock's chiming. It had taken her a while to

---

19 emprime (Bulg.)—printed cloth.

pick an outfit suitable for the occasion. Appearances were important. Especially in *their* case. Mrs. Bachvarova[20] was an energetic, well-adjusted middle-aged woman married to a well-respected, well-adjusted, and very successful scientist in the employ of the prestigious BAN.[21] As such, he enjoyed the privilege of being allowed to attend conferences abroad in the West. He was trusted. Mrs. Bachvarova was not permitted to accompany him on these trips, but she was the primary beneficiary of her husband's travels. It had to do with the clothes he brought back for her. But she was not trusted. Mr. Bachvarov was much older than his wife, and so he cared a lot about her and her wishes. Not that this had any bearing on the delicate situation they were in and the treatment they were subjected to based on trust. The point was that neither was a party member. Also, there was another fact to be considered: Dr. Bachvarov had acquired his PhD many years ago at the Sorbonne University, in Paris—an excellent university, highly regarded in his country, but, unfortunately, it was in the West, and that was not a highly regarded qualification at the present. However, he was successful in establishing himself as a very valuable specialist and was astute enough to know how to keep his dominance by different means, short of becoming a party member. So the trust he had been enjoying was rather like walking on thin ice.

Absorbed in her thoughts, Mrs. Bachvarova had reached the front door, failing to hear the sound generated by a key turning in the keyhole, and before she knew it the door flew open in front of her face, almost knocking her off her feet and pushing her back to the wall.

---

20 Bachvarova (Gram.)—a female family name characterized by the suffix "ova."
21 BAN—Bulgarian Academy of Science.

"Sorry," the young man uttered, startled by the silhouette framed in the opening of the doorway. He squeezed in, brushing against his mother. A young woman followed him closely—blushing, her eyes cast down. Mrs. Bachvarova remained at the spot with her back against the wall, holding the door open, her eyes following the couple, waiting. She motioned for her son to get back to her.

"Nedah called," she whispered, then turned around and pulled the door closed, leaving the young man standing inside facing the dark foyer. A few moments later he was back in the interior of the apartment, his face tensed up in a forced smile. He threw a quick look around the living room, then, as the sound of the closing door and the following footsteps reverberating on the mosaic floor of the stairway landing died out, headed straight to the corridor leading to the bedrooms, pulling the woman behind him, her coat and purse left in a heap on one of the chairs in the living room. Presently, the click emitted by the key turning in the bedroom door's keyhole was the only sound to interrupt the monotony of the grandfather clock's tick-tock echoing through the stillness.

Days, months passed…At a table squeezed in the far corner of Café Praga—far away from the windows—Nedah and Alex sat facing each other, smoking. The ashtray was full of cigarette butts, and the glasses full of cheap plum brandy were untouched. The twilight was fading quickly, and the pale light emitted by the street lights was taking over. It was the favorite time of day for Nedah, when all daily anxieties seemed to vanish, replaced by a sense of tranquility mixed with hopeful expectations. No urgency, no fear, no doubts.

"How are things with you?" said Alex.

"OK."

"Sorry I didn't call back. Was away…" he mumbled while pulling the cigarette stub from the side of his mouth. The smoke got into his eye, distorting his face into a familiar grimace. Nedah eyes fixed on his face, feeling a tug in her heart.

"Uh…Sorry…What did you say…Aha, you were away." She almost asked *Where,* but the word stuck in her throat. Instead, she heard herself mutter, "Never mind."

"What do you want me to do? Just tell me. I'll do whatever you want me to do…" He was leaning over the table, his face betraying an intense urgency.

"What do you mean?" The question was merely a rhetorical one, a way to gain some time, to let herself experience a momentary joy in the belief that there was hope, a possibility for happiness and future. And it was hers just for the asking, all the while knowing that this was the end.

"Do you still keep the photo?"

"Yes," he said.

He pulled out his wallet and held it open for her, displaying a picture.

"Not that one," Nedah retorted. Her eyes did not linger on the photo she recognized instantly by its size, the broken corner from handling the glossy paper, identical to the one she kept in her purse.

"This one," she said after a quick glance at the new one in his hand.

"Rip it up," she said, looking straight into his eyes. And he did, without hesitation and with his eyes fixed on hers. *So it was done.* It would do for a while. The relief was temporary and had to do with her mind-set: the craving for order as a substitute for stability in the chaos of her life. It was not a solution to the problem, and it was only meant to afford her a breathing space for a while until she was able to regain some strength.

"That is all?"

"Yes. That is all," she said calmly.

It was well after midnight when they stopped in front of the apartment building door. It was quiet as usual at this time of night, only a couple of hours before the street-washing crew would appear, dragging the rolls of water hoses spewing thick sheaves of water, turning the pavement shiny and permeating the air with freshness scented with the sweet smell of linden trees in bloom.

Places to Sleep

The sharp ring of the clock ripped through the quiet in the room. The thick padded cover of the bed flew off, and a man emerged with eyes still closed. He pressed the alarm clock's bell and dropped his feet to the floor. Automatically, he grabbed the pair of socks from the floor and pulled them onto his feet. After accomplishing the task, he rested for a moment while seated on the edge of the bed, half awake, his head heavy on his neck with a slowly dissipating fog of dreams. The room was dark, and the early morning light from the outside streaming through the white sheer window covers created a few gray spots. It was a portent of a dreary fall day. Suddenly the man dropped back on his back, pulled his feet clad in socks under the cover, and hugged the pillow.

A couple of hours later he was up, completely dressed, and determined. Through the panes of the window facing east, the visible patch of sky was gray, with a hint of yellow fog hanging over the low hills. A foul smell drifted from the outside into the room. It was a constant reminder of the proximity of the Kremikovtsi industrial complex, its presence magnified by fog or the heavy air on days like today. The man was busy emptying drawers, pulling clothes off the hangers in a wardrobe covered in cracked panels of veneer, and packing all the stuff into a large suitcase.

Presently, he stood on the platform built up along the streetcar tracks, waiting for the tram going in the opposite direction of his daily commute. The suitcase hung from his right arm. Today was the one-year anniversary of when he started working at Kremikovtsi after graduating from the university, as the fulfillment of the compulsory requirement at the end of his studies. Meanwhile, his diploma lay stored in some Ministry department, to be delivered to him at the end of the three-year term, as per requirement.

For the last few weeks he had been living with an increased sense of anxiety about the approaching event. The thought of having to go through the same dreary existence for two more years kept creeping into his consciousness, rendering his future unbearable. "Life is not supposed to be all misery." It was a thought that he could not shake off all day long while going about his duties, surrounded by the noise, breathing in and out the foul air of his workplace.

He had been struggling with the morning routine each morning of every working day all year long: awaken by the loud clock, the brief visit to the washroom, checking the weather outside, getting dressed mindlessly...Today, though, something had snapped, and without any further thought he had put an end to all that. It might be called a watershed moment in most people's lives, but for the man it felt like the most natural thing that had happened to him, finally. Ahead of him there was nothing to look forward to, and behind him there was nothing worth remembering.

The streetcar arrived exactly on schedule. This was remarkable, he thought as he entered the streetcar in front of him.

Winter had arrived. The streets were covered in snow. It was early afternoon. The air was sharp but sweet, and translucent. The man was walking along the sidewalk, accompanied by a young woman. Somebody was celebrating a name day.[22] During this time of the year, each day it

---

22 Name day is a tradition in some countries in Europe and Latin America that consists of celebrating a day of the year that is associated with one's given name. Name

seemed to be someone's name day time. The couple walked through an apartment building, passing by the elevator with a note hanging on its door, "out of order." As a matter of fact, the note was so old that nobody remembered the time when there was not one and the elevator had been working. The stain-covered paper was peeling from the grimy surface, its corners curled and the letters faded. Nobody paid attention to it, so it did not matter.

The man and his friend walked past the door and straight to the staircase. Five stories up, they stood in front of another grimy door. A loud noise of laughter, commotion, and music drifted out to the landing. A girl opened the door, pulled them in enthusiastically, and left them immediately—as soon as they entered the hall and she shut the door.

The party was in its full-blown intensity. The air was thick with cigarette smoke permeated by the sharp smell of brandy. A couple of loud conversations competed with the sound of the rock-and-roll melody drifting from the tape player for the attention of the few showing interest.

Time passed, and the party was now winding down. Most of the people had left, and only two couples remained: an older one and him and her. The hostess was starting to clean up, rushing to the kitchen carrying dirty dishes and glasses, wiping spots with damp rags. The music had stopped about an hour ago, after the phone rang and the hostess's voice could be heard apologizing to someone on the other end of the connection before turning off the tape player. Meanwhile, she kept throwing surreptitious looks at the two remaining couples, unable to bring herself to show them the door. Finally, with a sigh, she opened

---

days in Bulgaria are almost always associated with Bulgarian Eastern Orthodox celebrations. According to the tradition, guests are supposed to come uninvited and the person who has the celebrated name is supposed to be prepared to treat everyone. The celebration is similar to a birthday.

the door to the bedroom and closed it behind her, leaving the guests to themselves. The last glimpse she got was of one couple sprawled across the chesterfield and the other engaged in arm wrestling. Her face screwed up at the odd scene.

The pale winter sun was slowly emerging from the horizon when the man and the young woman stepped out from the front door of the apartment building. The streets were empty. The sharp sensation of the cold pinching their faces felt refreshing after the night spent in the room, growing cold and with air still rancid from the lingering smell of cigarette smoke. The woman's shoulders shivered and the man threw his arm around her, pulling her close to him. The couple continued their slow walk as one—oblivious, lost in the empty streets of a chilly early morning.

The city was coming alive, with people scurrying along the streets, crowding the bus and streetcar shelters, and climbing into the packed vehicles, pushing and shoving one another. Small neighborhood stores selling yogurt were opening. The man and the young woman stopped at the entrance of one of them and gave each other a hug and a peck on the cheek. "Thank you! I'll give you a call later in the day," the man said to the young woman before he entered the store for a breakfast of a bowl of yogurt and gevrek.[23] Inside, the morning ritual was in full blast. Pensioners in a long line, big bowls of different shapes in their hands, were patiently waiting their turn to get their share of the daily milk in its different varieties. The man picked up one of the small containers of individual servings on display on the counter and a fresh gevrek from a basket full of all kinds of rolls, buns, and banichki,[24] and left the fare next to the man

---

23   gevrek (Tur.)—bagel.
24   banichki—snack made of filo dough with cheese filing.

serving the customers in the line. Then he took a seat at a small table by the window.

The young woman, just a friend, sharing hard times with Svetozar, continued on her way to who knows where.

A Brief Bio Regarding Svetozar's Friend…

Her name was Mariana. Svetozar met Mariana when he started work at Kremikovtsi. They met in the apartment where they both lived in separate, rented rooms. It was late at night when they bumped into each other in the dark hallway, in front of the washroom. Both were in a hurry and somewhat impaired. The moment Svetozar realized that the stranger in the dark was a lady, he moved away, apologized for his clumsiness, and held the door open for her. Mariana was shocked by the treatment she had just received, one she had never experienced before—being treated as a lady rather than as a conscientious worker, which she was, as she had proved by achieving the status of Udarnichka[25]and keeping it. As a matter of fact, she was proud of it. Mariana was physically strong, of course, and sensible, but not sensitive about how she was perceived by every Sullyo and Pullyu[26] with an opinion. She shared a room with another girl from the same provincial town from which she came. But that did not make her a friend, just a roommate. The place where she was born and raised was a small one, smack in the middle of a picturesque valley surrounded by big mountains. In spite of its designation as a town, its population was closer to peasantry by occupation. Most worked on the local cooperative farm. Her father was a mechanic who fixed the machinery of the local collective

25 Udarnichka (Bul.)—rank of shock-worker won by exceeding the production quotas.
26 Sullyo and Pullyu (Bulg. slang)—Chump and Clump (approximation).

farm, and her mother was one of the few female tractor operators. And this accounted for Mariana's choice of employment as a factory worker. Working around machinery and the stench of metal was in her blood.

The friendship between the two was a marvel to some. What was this quiet, urban polyglot doing by chumming with the inarticulate, provincial, proletarian factory worker? And when the news broke that Svetozar had left abruptly, some had their suspicions. Also, that precluded any possibility of Mariana offering any accommodations to Svetozar. Not that he would have accepted…But she did not abandon her friend, and did all she could to help. Even if it was just providing him with company in an unusual scheme.

§

It was summertime. The streets around as well as the square between Hotel Balkan and the Central Universal Store were lively with tourists from the provinces coming to the capital city, curious as well as disoriented and lost. Among them, though, were a few foreign travelers: businessmen residing in the hotel, or occasional expats. Both kinds were easy to spot by their attire, and most of all by their smiling faces. In fact, this was the most striking difference between the two categories of pedestrians seen around. The man, dressed in jeans and t-shirt, was walking nonchalantly among the crowd, with his hands pushed inside his pockets and a friendly smile masquerading his sharp concentration on the foreign tourists. Occasionally he would approach a male and whisper without any visible change in his countenance: "Dollars for levs— exchange at a good rate." Most passed him without giving him as much as a glance, but occasionally some stopped, and after a brief exchange of words, a surreptitious exchange of bundles of banknotes followed. The nonchalant young man would quickly slip away and disappear from the scene.

It was getting late, and Tony was losing patience as he waited when he heard the voice coming from behind him. He turned around to face the young man standing awkwardly and staring intently at him.

"Sorry for being late," said Svetozar.

"Never mind," said Tony. His eyes were fixed on the suitcase hanging from the grip of the man's hand in front of him.

"Going someplace?" he asked.

"Hmm…Not really…Looking for a place to stay…"

"No problem," Tony said.

The room was dark, and the sparse furniture was hard to distinguish in the dusk of the moonlight streaming inside through the semi-circular window. A couch, a single bed, a small table pushed against the wall, and a couple of chairs filled the room. A door, now closed, indicated the entrance to another room. It was Mrs. Filipova's bedroom, often referred to as *Madam Filipova's boudoir* by her son Tony, a vague reference to a life once experienced in better circumstances. At the present, Mrs. Filipova was not around, and there was no food in the place either. Also, there was no need to go look for it in the communal kitchen, as nobody left any food there. It was partially for fear of the cockroaches that came in droves in the night, emerging from the places where they had spent the day hiding from the light. So Svetozar dropped his suitcase on the floor by the couch, hung the raincoat he had been carrying on his arm on one of the hooks attached to the door, and walked out onto the staircase's platform to wait for Tony to lock up the place.

Quickly, they disappeared in the maze of streets in search of an open tripe shop.

It was late, past midnight, when the two returned to the attic in the house on the corner. The room was still dark, but a ribbon of light emanated from the space under the door to *Madam Filipova's boudoir*. Behind the door, Mrs. Filipova was in bed, reclining on a pile of pillows, covered halfway up her chest, holding the soiled covers of the New Testament in her hands—reading.

It was in the early dawn of the next day when Tony squeezed himself from under the covers of his bed and walked to the door of his mother's room. On the way, he threw a perfunctory look at the bulging pile of blankets on the couch hiding its occupant. He opened and closed the door, taking a great care not to disturb the soundly sleeping man, but proceeded to his mother's bed with an eager and sure stride.

Tony's face had darkened and his eyes shone through the mist he was trying hard to conceal. His mother was in the reoccurring state of hibernation she fell into after each of the events like her last disappearance in the previous few days. On such occasions, her behavior could be categorized best as one defying the natural cycle of existence in consecutive awake and sleep states. Instead, she seemed to function in an uninterrupted haze, day and night—never thoroughly awake, never truly asleep. It was only in her presence, during times like that, that Tony allowed himself to show his true nature and how close his inner self was to hers, and how misleading was the entire cheerful and easygoing façade he carried around all day long.

"Mother, how did it go?"

"As usual…He is all right…"The answer was preceded by a long silence and was categorical. It was to be understood that she was greatly exhausted and that the conversation had reached its conclusion. Then she pulled herself up, just enough to twist her upper body and swing her arm to reach under the pillow. Silently, Tony watched her retrieve the blue envelope from its hiding place and hand it to him. On his way back to his room, he opened and closed the door with the same care as he had a few minutes ago.

The story was old, painful, and complicated. It was a secret that was steeped in hopelessness and helplessness, but one that had to be maintained at all costs, for it was the foundation on which his family existence depended, as well as his future. The secret ruled their lives.

The sun was shining and there was a slight wind. The human traffic in front of Hotel Balkan was substantial; the business was good. Tony had glanced at his watch before he moved away from the thick of the crowd, as far as the time to pull out the cigarette pack from his jean's pocket took him to. Next, he stopped, pulled out a cigarette lighter, and lit the cigarette he had already placed between his lips, surrounded by his cupped fingers in a protective manner. After the first exhale he renewed his brisk walk. By the time he reached Café Levski, the drag on Rakovska Street had reached considerable volume. At one of the tables next to the window, Svetozar was seated, absorbed in the newspaper spread in front of him.

"Hello," Tony said, standing next to the table. "Do you mind if we move to another table? There is one by the wall, in the corner."

"No problem," said Svetozar, without sending even a glance to the location while folding the newspaper. Somewhat sheepishly, he followed Tony to the table in the far corner.

"What are you going to have?" he asked.

"A small cognac," Tony said.

"Two small cognacs," Svetozar called to the waitress passing by with a tray full of dirty glasses.

"Right," she called back, without stopping by the table or acknowledging in any way the customer ordering the drinks. She knew all of the regulars and their tastes. The local Pliska cognac was the most popular drink among the younger customers. It was a different story with the older people. The pensioner's standard was tea with lemon, and the most affordable item available on the short menu.

"Thanks for your hospitality," Svetozar said in a low voice as he twirled the glass filled with cognac between the palms of his hands. He paused. "Have to tell you something that should remain between us."

He brought the glass to his lips and swallowed some of the yellow liquid before he continued.

"As a matter of fact, I need your help. I would need some foreign currency. Dollars, preferably..." After failing to elicit a response from his friend, who had kept his silence while staring him right in the eyes, he blurted, "I am going on an excursion to Greece and will need some dollars..."

"But of course," Tony responded finally. "Wait till we get home." He paused. "Tell me, how are you going to do it?" he asked, with a hint of hesitation in his voice.

A small crowd had gathered in front of Hotel Balkan, waiting for the arrival of a bus going south. Most were tourists from the neighboring Greece. This was evident from the kind of luggage they had placed at their feet or had hanging from their arms, from the quality of their shoes and the fashion of their clothes, from the stickers on their suitcases, and, most extraordinarily, even from the expressions on their faces that set them apart from the locals. Also, this was what made the man and his large suitcase stick out in the crowd as someone who did not belong anywhere, an impression created by the demeanor of someone trying hard to blend, to become invisible.

Finally, the driver emerged from the hotel, where he had gone to take a break and fortify himself with some food and drink before starting on the long journey along badly maintained roads winding in the shadows of mountains on both sides. As the filled-to-capacity bus started slowly pulling from the parking spot, the wide sidewalk of Boulevard Stambolijski running into the square Sveta Nedelia came into view. Standing in a casual pose, his hands shoved into the pockets of his ironed jeans, head slightly kinked to one side, stood a young man, waiting for clients. A changer.[27]

---

27 changer—someone involved in the illegal practice of currency exchange.

From the corner of his eye, Svetozar could see his friend Tony. And so he did. For the last time.

About four hours into the ride, the bus came to a stop. The driver turned around in his seat and made the following announcement: "To all passengers! Prepare for crossing into the Border Security zone. Those traveling on Bulgarian internal passports need to show their security clearance document by the DS of the Ministry of the Interior. Those without clearance should disembark in the area designated for this purpose. The remaining passengers will have their passports examined by the Border Security."

As the bus stopped at the designated area, Svetozar stood up from his seat, pulled down the raincoat he had placed in the net strip running over the row of seats, and stepped down from the bus. The driver had already opened the door of the baggage compartment at the bottom of the vehicle. Svetozar pulled his suitcase and headed away, toward the village center. As soon as the bus disappeared from his sight, he changed direction and headed toward the hills. It was a pleasantly warm day. The ground was dry, and the area was covered with bushes thick with ripe berries. Svetozar picked a place away from any visible paths, laid the suitcase on the ground, unlocked the catch, and pulled out the backpack squeezed inside it.

He sat on the warm earth, resting his body on the bag and the empty suitcase next to him. Then he closed his eyes in wait for the darkness of the long night ahead to envelop the earth, hoping, meanwhile, to get some rest from all the exhausting tension of the long day and clear his mind. He had already reassured himself that all maps and documents were there by pressing the palm of his hand over one of the compartments of his backpack until he felt the particular feeling of paper resisting behind the fabric. Also, he had taken a look at the empty suitcase, his face and eyes screwing up at the sight of the now useless piece of luggage that had to be discarded discretely in a spot hidden from people's gaze, as soon as possible, somewhere before he reached the border.

§

Many years, perhaps decades, had passed since I'd seen Svetozar. It was in the old country, long after graduation from the school we both had attended and the last time we had met at the house on the corner when he was staying with Tony. It was the early 1980s, and not long before the fall of the Wall, the one both of us had crossed, running away from the claustrophobic place we lived in, a place covered in the pollution of yellow, stinky smog spewed out of thousands of chimneys—a testament of the mindless pursuit of glory. Also, a place full of walls planted in people's minds and hearts. But I am digressing...

It was springtime in Paris. It was difficult for me to imagine any other place on earth better than that. The smells, the sights, the sounds, all were overwhelming. My companion and I were sitting at a table in a café on Champs-Élysées, enjoying the ambiance and the architectural beauty of the nearby Petit Palais. We were so taken by all that we were seeing and experiencing at the moment that we were discussing the possibility of moving there. It was not the first time we had contemplated a similar move, and certainly we were letting the fancy have its way, with an eagerness and sincerity we felt as 100 percent genuine at the moment. And as we kept expanding on our future plans, we started to dissect the daily lives we would have. One point my companion made was the fact that we had no friends living permanently in this charming urban paradise to share our happiness with, except each other, of course. It was a very poignant point indeed, and here I had this sudden revelation: Somewhere in my notebook I must have been carrying around the address and number of my classmate and friend from the old country, an intelligent, friendly man who had (by now) somehow made it to Paris. I'd gotten the address from a friend who lived in the house on the corner. This was really a stroke of luck in more than one way. First, people in my and his situation, due to the manner in which they had left the country, did not keep in touch with friends in the motherland for fear of the censorship and of bringing the wrath of the Internal Security on them. All those miserable circumstances aside, it was a great moment when I succeeded in finding the phone number, locating a public telephone, and finally even recognizing the faintly familiar voice I now heard through the telephone.

"Hello. Is this Svetozar?" I said, conscious of the silly smile nobody was going to see across the ether.

"Yes, it is," the voice answered in a tentative tone, which invoked a picture of a face without a smile.

That same day, the three of us met in a small cozy restaurant, where we were among Frenchmen and no tourists. It was a lovely evening. I was glad that my companion got along well with my former classmate and friend. We shared a lot, laughed a lot, but contrary to our expectations, Svetozar abruptly stood up after a glance at his watch. It left an impression that he wanted to be someplace else at the particular time. Frankly, I was getting annoyed. But then he said, "If you have no other plans for tomorrow, I would like to invite you to come to my place. I'll pick you up from your hotel and will take you there."

"Great!" we answered enthusiastically as we shook hands.

"Till tomorrow then…" he said, rather meekly.

As we both watched him going away with a slightly sheepishly gait, I could not resist the temptation to wrap it all neatly with a statement relating to our previous conversation and considerations that brought about this surprising reunion in the first place.

"It is going to be an education," I said.

My companion smiled with satisfaction.

The following day, around six o'clock, we found ourselves in a place we would have never imagined seeing only yesterday. It was Paris, but had little to do with the part of the city we fell in love with the day before. It was a bit shabby; the buildings were in great need of repair, although the architecture evoked visions of old grandeur. The street was full of litter, and by the looks on the faces of the people moving around absentmindedly and quickly, as people do when in a familiar place, one could surmise the middle-class standing of the inhabitance. The ambience was one of isolation and slightly depressing. We got there on foot and partly by the subway. At one point of our journey to his place, Svetozar stopped abruptly and pointed out in the direction to the west.

"From here you can see the Eiffel Tower. Here it is, in the sunshine during this time of day." His face had acquired a glow that struck me in a strange way. *Hmm...Just as the Eifel Tower!*

"Got the place because of that sight," Svetozar continued.

What a dreamer... The thought crossed my mind.

We entered a small garden with a path covered in flagstones. The entrance to the building was difficult to distinguish from the low windows and a couple of doors serving a purpose that was hard to fathom. A narrow staircase came to view behind one of those doors. There was an elevator, but it was only for two passengers—too small for all three of us to squeeze in—so we decided to take the stairs to the third floor. In front of another indistinguishable door, Svetozar stopped, pulled a key chain from his pocket, and unlocked the door.

"Hello, anyone here?" he called in French.

Immediately a shadow of a man appeared from somewhere behind the short hallway, quickly approaching us with an extended hand.

"Yes. Yes…Here I am," he said cheerfully, in French. With that comment, my capacity of comprehension of the language was depleted.

"This is Maurice," Svetozar said in French first and then repeated in English.

"We can continue our communications in English, *n'est-ce pa?*"[28]

"Of course, of course…" Maurice said.

But who was Maurice? I was beginning to feel the curiosity build up in me. And there were clues. Many. The place was immaculate, furnished tastefully; the walls were covered with art. I even managed to take a quick peek into the only other room through the door left open, a bedroom in semidarkness in spite of a window, covered by drapes of thick, plush fabric.

"Oh, do you mind if I look through the window to see the view?" I said, and before anybody could say anything, I rushed into the room and pulled the drapes open. In front of me, no farther than a meter away, was a red brick wall. Maurice was standing by my side, smiling. Too embarrassed to say anything, I turned around and went back into the adjacent room, but not before taking note of the beautiful bed cover and artistically arranged pillows. So far the signals were mixed in my mind.

A Story about Svetozar's Mother

Svetozar's mother, or Mrs. Stoimenova, considered herself a modern woman. Urbane. Educated. She looked the part too. She was good-looking, rather handsome, if you know what I mean, and a proud mother of a smart and polite, if a bit chubby, boy. There was nothing he could not do as far as academics and art, although he was a bit too timid for his mother's taste. His teachers liked him too because he was one of those students who make them proud, as it is entirely logical to attribute some

---

28 *n'est-ce pas?* (Fr.)—isn't it so?

of the success of students to the greatness of their teachers, no? Svetozar was not one of the charming types or the more sports-oriented unruly rascals some teachers seem to develop a weakness for. But, he made them proud. Although, as I mentioned earlier, he was too meek at times.

So Svetozar went through school like a breeze. But when the time arrived for decisions to be made regarding what comes next, things started to get complicated. He had already mastered French, German, English, Russian, Italian, and, of course, his native tongue. With the knowledge of so many languages, there was no sense in studying linguistics or any other specialty related to this area at the university. In fact, for a while, he wanted to be a writer. But it did not work out. As far as his personality development was concerned, there were issues. He was too quiet, too friendly, and had no girlfriend. His mother wanted her son to be manly. And that is how Svetozar ended up studying engineering, chemical engineering, which was very popular at the time and encouraged for the future. There were many plants to be built and managed for chemical fertilizers, such nitric/nitrogen fertilizers. And being an engineer was a manly thing. And that was good. At the end of his studies, Svetozar was sent to spend his three years of compulsory practice to Kremikovtsi, the most impressive touted achievement in the economic development of his country. As it happened, though, he had to move to a rented room close to the complex because of the distance he had to travel if he remained in his parents' place. And what about buying a car? It simply was not done. One day, though, Svetozar couldn't take it anymore. But why didn't he go home? Another simple impossibility: He could not face his mother and tell her what he had discovered about himself. He found jobs doing translations and he pretended to have become manly. His mother was too glad to believe the lies. But it was not an easy life for Svetozar. There were only so many people to offer him a place to sleep for a prolonged time and so much danger...Those were the times of housing shortage in the capital city, collectivization in the countryside, and labor camps for the undesirable.

So one day he took a bus in front of Hotel Balkan, going south, and was lucky to make it.

§

It was a lovely evening. Maurice had prepared an excellent dinner. The food was complemented by excellent wine, and the presentation was impeccable. The conversation was lighthearted but also stimulating, drifting into discussions about morality, social justice, and other highly relevant subjects. The time Svetozar spent with Tony at the house on the corner was remembered by the two of us, and commentaries were pondered upon about the strange situation with Tony's missing father, whom both of us had seen in a photo in a beautiful and ornate frame placed on top of a bookshelf in his mother's room. We met one more time before we flew back home, but we kept in touch and remained close. So this was the beginning of our rekindled beautiful friendship, to paraphrase a famous movie. We did not move to Paris, but we never abandoned the idea. It was just a postponement. Svetozar and Maurice remained together for a long time.

At the end of the 1980s, Mrs. Stoimenova visited her son. She had been waiting for years for a piece of news from her son that would bring joy to her heart. It was not anymore a question only about manliness, but about posterity: Where are the babies? It seems that after being badgered heavily for a considerable time by his mother on this subject, Svetozar had finally let her know where he stood. It seems that Mrs. Stoimenova had not been able to see the obvious truth about the relationship between her son and his pal and had accepted her son's initial explanation: Maurice was just a friend in need of a place to sleep.

Discovering the true nature of their liaison left her in shock and disbe-lief. There were no more reasonable doubts left to feed the denial. The situation became intolerable, and there was no solution. Maurice left the apartment, but it was just a bandage, a temporary measure.

By then Mrs. Stoimenova was in advanced age and suffering from a number of ailments. This contributed to Svetozar's chagrin. To com-pensate for the heartache he was causing her and to alleviate his own feelings of guilt, he did something very common: He showered her with presents. After a year-long intensely emotional visit, Mrs. Stoimenova decided that she had had enough and was getting ready to return to her place back home, where she would be taken care of by her spinster niece, the daughter of her younger sister.

Mrs. Stoimenova passed away suddenly. It was her heart. Thankfully it was not a protracted illness. It had happened only a couple of days before she was to take the flight back home. It was a heavy blow for Svetozar. He felt devastated, torn by guilt, sorrow, and confusion. The funeral was grand. The music was exquisite: the "Humming Chorus" from the *Madame Butterfly* opera by G. Puccini. Lots of people showed, and at some point during the service, he became overwhelmed and had to be taken away.

A couple of months after the funeral, I received a package from Paris. The return address belonged to Svetozar Stoimenov. It was with some trepidation that I opened the large box, with no idea and expecta-tions of what would I find inside it. On top of the layers of soft paper the object was placed in—a sign of the special care with which the sender had handled the contents—there was a thank-you card. As I pulled out the last layer of the fine packaging material, I experienced a feeling hard to describe: overwhelmed, touched, thankful, and, of course, surprised. In front of my eyes appeared an item of women's attire: a lovely, elegant mink stole from the 1940s era. It was his mom's. And he wanted me to have it! As far as the thank-you card text, besides the usual, there was a reminder that we were always welcome to visit him and Maurice in Paris and not to worry about accommodations. We would always have a place to sleep there.

It Is All about "Happy Endings"

The shopping mall near the area famous for its Eastern European ethnic population buzzed with heavy activity during the lunch hour, as usual. Singles, couples, and small groups of people meandered through the crowds, searching for an empty spot on a bench or a place to squeeze in at already-occupied tables in the food court. It was noisy, and the air was permeated with a variety of spices evocative of different cuisines from all over the world, as well as the fragrances of all kind of brands of perfumes, deodorants, and beauty products. Laughter and music mixed in a cacophony of sound. The ambience was of excitement and happiness, created by the crowd of mostly young people. But not exclusively. Every day, regardless of weather conditions that included all four seasons, a bunch of oldies and middle-agers lucky enough to be early retirees could be seen leisurely reclining in their chairs, pushed back to a considerable distance away from the tables, stretching their legs and sipping their consecutive daily cups of coffee. There were no heavy conversations and loud discussions during this particular time. It could have been the noise that discouraged such activity, or most probably it was a sort of intermezzo when people-watching and cheery relaxation generated enough energy to be spent in the aftermath: arguing, complaining, and even throwing a tantrum or two in indignation.

Mr. Stephan Filipov was one of the permanent members of the bunch. Most of the regulars were single men. And most had gone through long and torturous journeys they did not like to discuss with whoever happened to drop by for a cup of coffee in a public place— although all had strong convictions they loved talking about with their fellow believers dedicated to the same causes. As far as their private lives were concerned, not much was shared. All those complicated lives during those difficult times of their youth…Stephen Filipov's story, if there was one anyone knew about, was torturous and painful indeed. But hardly anyone would have guessed it when talking to him in the shopping mall's food court get-togethers with old chums.

Stephan Filipov was born into an old and well-respected family at the beginning of the twentieth century. At the time, the country he was delivered into was still going through the painful process of establishing itself as an independent, modern European one. Patriotism, education, politics, and interest in different kinds of ideologies were very much in vogue. It was a turbulent and exciting time to live in. There was also another peculiarity: The capital of this newly minted country, Sofia, was more akin to the status of parvenu among the bigger, more centrally located cities of the kingdom. The best city, Veliko Tarnovo, the old and last capital of the most glorious period in the history of the nation (if we can speak about such a thing when referring to the subject), the charming Veliko Tarnovo, was bypassed in the process of selecting the new capital. But I am digressing.

It could be said that much of the intelligentsia of the time originated from the provincial cities rather than from the capital one. And to the point: Mr. S. Filipov was born in Plovdiv in the year of 1910. He received his university education in Germany (the specifics of the exact place, university, and area of expertise are irrelevant, as none of those plays any role of importance in the following story). After graduating and getting his papers, he packed his belongings, put his diploma in a beautiful box, and returned to his native land, where immediately he got involved in his father's business of import–export and started enjoying the life of a single, unattached dandy. He was a handsome and usually stylishly dressed man, with an attractive, shining personality. Also, he was not in a hurry to get married. This was not unusual, though, when regarded in the light of one peculiarity of those times: the trend of educated men with good prospects to marry later to pretty girls often a decade younger in age. But at one point in time he found *the one* and took her to the altar. And, of course, she was beautiful and a decade his junior. There was already a war going on, but Plovdiv was still a peaceful place to live in. It was the 1940s, and a big calamity was on the way: the air raids over the capital city. Evacuees from Sofia were drifting into the provinces, but in the cities with a larger population, like Plovdiv, they got lost, hardly visible. There were rumors, but nothing to prove them right. Eventually, the war came to an end, but the consequences of it were still to be felt for those were not directly related to the war itself. But indirectly they were. And very much so.

So life was good for the new couple. A son, Anton, was born.

But then all went wrong…

Of course, things with the world had been going wrong for a long time, but I am talking about this family that had somehow survived relatively unscathed by a war but was devastated by what came after it. It had to do with Mr. S. Filipov's political views and affiliations. Apparently Mr. Filipov had acquired some of those during his studies abroad, or who knows where. It does not seem logical for a son helping his father run an import–export business to fall for the peasants and their cause. But isn't it possible for a man to develop greater sensitivity to causes bigger than his station in society? And this was the case with Mr. S. Filipov.

For a while, life for the family was good, and the future seemed to be too because they were in the winning camp. The peasants had united with the proletariat and become the rulers of the nation—but not for all with political affiliation to one of the factions the agrarian union was breaking into. For the followers of Nikola Petkov, it lasted for a very short time in the historical sense, but it ended up in an eternity of misery for the Filipov family.

On September 23, 1947, Nikola Petkov, one of the leaders of BZNS,[29] was executed; following a show trial without legal representation or evidence, he was found guilty of espionage and hanged. He was buried in an unknown grave, just as the bodies of over a hundred representatives of the National Assembly tried by the People's Court in 1944 were disposed of. Although there was one difference, in the carrying out the sentence—it was in the manner of the execution. Hanging over a hundred people would have been a very slow and tiresome task.

The aftermath of this episode in the establishment of the system of the dictatorship of the proletariat, in fact, put fear in people's minds and the paranoia that poisoned the everyday lives of ordinary citizens. Who was safe if Nikola Petkov wasn't?

The arrests followed; people were sent to the Belyane labor camp. The supporters of Nikola Petkov were branded as traitors and the enemy. An exodus of political refugees ensued. Most were young and single. But there were a few who left their families behind and started on a journey they could have never imagined not long before. The reason for that was simple; they believed that soon they would be back. The wives and the children were to be spared the hardships. The secrecy had to be preserved to protect those left behind from retaliation. So many tales were told, many epic stories were created and spread.

Stephan Filipov ended up in a place far away, beyond the ocean. Meanwhile, back home, his wife and child moved to the capital city of Sofia. It was the biggest city in the country with the largest population—easy to get lost in the multitude of people. As long as one knew how to keep his mouth shut and be a patriotic citizen, of course.

---

29 BZNS—Bulgarian Agrarian National Union.

The years rolled by. Mr. Filipov made ends meet somehow and was able even to send some money to his son and wife. He urged them to keep the secret, not to share anything with anybody. Some men in his situation remarried, and who was to stop them? But Stephan Filipov never did. And nobody knew where he was drawing all that strength from. His son, Tony, had no memories of his father, but kept dreaming that one day he would see him. His wife suffered, lost in her loneliness and her devotion to her son. From time to time, she would take the train and travel to Plovdiv to pick up a letter from her husband. The letter was addressed to her brother-in-law—Stephan's younger sibling. Those were not the usual letters of relatives exchanging news full of details related to their daily lives or commenting on world events one read about in the newspapers or heard over the radio, or saw on television in later times. On the contrary, those were mundane letters, from an old friend from long ago—hopefully dull enough to put to sleep the censorship apparatchik reading them.

The fear and paranoia of bringing harm to his family ran deep in Stephan Filipov's mind. So deep, in fact, that he would never even send some news about himself to his son by mouth through people traveling back home. How could he be sure that those people could be trusted? Who were they spying for? The compatriots he met in the church he attended kept wondering about his personal life—the one he had left behind. Did he leave a family? Was he divorced? He made no effort to hide his political affiliations and loyalties that brought about the situation he now found himself in. But people wanted to know more. Some whispered strange stories…

And this was the unknown story of one of the bunch of oldies who gathered faithfully every day of the year, regardless of weather conditions, in the food court of the shopping mall at the end of the late 1980s. It was just before another momentous event was about to happen. And it happened. In 1989. And it was spectacular. For a while…

Radka Yakimov

The Strange Story about How to Kill a Monk

Let us start with the obvious question of why anyone would try to sneak back across a border he had crossed only recently, risking his life. Well, this would have been a good question if one had a choice. But choice was not something Stephan Filipov had. And at this point of the story regarding the trials and tribulations of the person just mentioned, I'll stop using any appellation in front of his name. Clearly he was not a *Comrade,* for otherwise he would have not been in the predicament he was at the time I am describing. And as far as *Mister* goes, he was not that anymore either, for *Mister* implies some respectability in society and recognition as a member of the human race. But Stephan Filipov lost all of his respectability and rights as a person once he entered the refugee camp, which was full of people from all over. And not all of them were what they pretended to be, I am sorry to say.

I'll skip the story about the trials and tribulations Stephan Filipov experienced during the escape across the border and how he ended up in the refugee camp. This kind of story was not of great interest to his compatriots who ended up in the same corner of the world and attended the same church he did, and what I am talking about is a story whispered by those very people. And, as most of them had gone through the same trials and tribulations anyway, it was not unusual that they did not find anything strange in such a story. But how many had gone back? And how many had gone through such a nightmare as to kill a monk? For it is one thing to eliminate an ideological enemy, and another thing to commit a sin.

It was a dark night and the sky above was illuminated by thousands, maybe millions, of stars, looking brighter and bigger than anyone from the small band of men would have seen till then. There was nothing to distinguish any of them from the men passing through those mountains at night and during the day, all year round. The most remarkable characteristic would be that they were even less noticeable somehow. Or wished to be. One of them was a local, and that could be the explanation for the confidence with which all the men strode through the terrain. Also, all of them had gun holsters tied around their waists, and this certainly added to the sense of confidence and courage one could muster under such circumstances. In the distance, the thick walls of a monastery were visible. Its doors stayed firmly shut, and the little flickering lights streaming through the small windows of the monks' cells were extinguished at that hour. It was already midnight, and there was not much time left to waste—only a few short hours were left till the monks would be up and starting their daily routine with a prayer. And among them was one monk who was to be no more after the sunrise. If nothing went wrong. This man of the cloth, though, was not what he was supposed to be, like many other folks in the place and time described in this strange story. The man wearing the simple garment of God's servant was, in fact, serving a very anti-God DS,[30] a branch of the central one located on Moskovska 5.[31] And he had to be eliminated. And those are not my words, but the words used in the documentation and order papers issued for the purpose of that action.

The band of men reached the monastery walls on time. All had gone well and according to plan. There was nothing else left for the men but to wait. So they found a most secluded spot close to the thick and beautiful (just a brief poetic digression to dispel the gruesome overall picture of what is to come) monastery doors surrounded by bushes and wildflowers and lay on the ground with guns drawn. Time passed slowly until the faint sound of a rooster's crow drifted from behind the stone walls

---

30 DS (Darzhavna sigurnost) (Bul.)—National Security.

31 Moskovska 5 (address)—the headquarters of the Metropolitan Police Department at the Ministry of Internal Affairs and the National Security Committee.

of the monastery, breaking the stillness of the night. It was time. The tension was mounting. The men stood up and took positions. All of their eyes were fixed on the thick monastery walls. Finally, the doors started to move, opening slowly. A shadow of a man drifted through the opening and began advancing toward the spot where the band of men hid. A volley of shots was heard. The shadow disappeared as a man dressed in black appeared on the gravel road leading out of the monastery.

Quickly, the doors shut. The band of men darted in a direction opposite to the one they had arrived from a couple of hours earlier. Another rooster's crow was heard, followed by silence. All was quiet on the eastern side of the monastery wall. The only visible reminder was that of a monk and his bag, down on the ground in front of the beautiful monastery walls. The bag was full of lists of names and reports typed on a typewriter, apparently damaged by overuse of the letter "E." And don't ask me what all that was about.

Anyway, it was a strange story, as I said in the beginning, and personally I do not believe it ever happened. But this was not the case with some of the compatriots of Stephan Filipov—the ones sharing the lunch hour in a shopping mall far away from home.

§

The moving truck, parked by the sidewalk curb in front of the house on the corner, was half full with old furniture brought down from the top floor—the original attic of the house—by a couple of burly men. The narrow wooden stairs emitted a sharp squeaking sound, louder than in earlier times, at every step taken by one of the laborers. Navigating through the winding staircase was a slow, cumbersome, time-consuming operation; it was obvious from the sight of profuse sweat glistening and trickling all over the exposed skin of both men. A middle-aged man kept showing up, moving from the interior to the sidewalk with his arms full of packages, fussing over their safe placement. Judging by the fastidious care he was displaying in handling every object, it was apparent that he was the person moving out of the premises and the owner of all that stuff.

An elderly lady appeared from one of the side streets, using a cane for support. Her body swayed with each of her steps, in an apparent effort to maintain balance. Her face was beaming with a smile—incongruous, considering the difficulties she was experiencing.

"Hello, Tony," she chirped cheerfully. "Moving time, eh?" she said as she slowed the pace of her walk and turned her head to face the man.

"Yes, it's moving time," Tony said, without much enthusiasm.

"Too bad your poor mother did not live to see it…" the old woman muttered as she moved her eyes away from the man and continued walking with resumed pace toward the entrance of the house on the corner. At the doorway, she stopped, straightened her posture, and turned around to face Tony again. With one hand firmly pushing against the doorframe and the other waving in the air, the walking stick emphasizing each of her words, she said in a firm voice, "And don't forget to call on me as soon as you settle down. Would like to have you with your family and father over for coffee. Have a question for him. Where was he during all those years?"

"Will do, will do…" Tony said with a smile.

Meanwhile, the old lady had turned around already and continued toward the first steps of the winding staircase, puffing and grimacing in expectation of the difficult and long climb ahead of her. She could hear Tony's strong voice behind her calling loudly to someone, "Hey, tell the guys to wait for a while till the lady gets in her flat."

Moskovska 5 and the Broken Marriage

The darkened beerhall of Restaurant "Bulgaria"—located under the restaurant on the ground level—was empty except for one table. The popular dining hall was part of the compound housed in the elegant multistory building of Hotel Bulgaria, situated in the most prestigious area of the city, and close to the former Tsar's Palace—now turned into an art gallery. It was the interval between lunch and dinnertime—too late for the first and too early for the latter. However, the place was never closed for customers—open all day long. Probably this was on account of the foreign visitors who favored the hotel. Hotel guests do not live on the customary schedules people follow in everyday circumstances, no? Hotel Bulgaria's reputation as the most fashionable place in town was passed by word of mouth, and so far it had been working. Advertising was not part of the system. It was a capitalistic evil. There were very few Western business capitalists coming to the country, but lately there were an increasing number of tourists attracted to the newly developed resorts by the Black Sea.

The man of the couple occupying the table in the beerhall was one of those. The other one was Vera. She looked changed to a point that it was difficult for some of her friends to recognize her after her ordeal a couple of years earlier. It was not so much her looks that had been altered somehow; it was something coming from within her inner self. Her chin had become square; the expression of her eyes had hardened, but in a good way—direct, confident, determined. The man was good-looking and fashionably dressed—the type of the well-preserved recognizable northern Italian male. The conversation was in French interspersed with Italian words.

"*Cara mia*,"[32] the man was saying, "it makes no difference indeed. I found the entire conversation totally ridiculous, and I told them so. It is my business whom I would marry. It is a personal matter."

The meal placed over the white tablecloth in front of each was simple: kashkaval-pane with fried potatoes on the side and two glasses of white wine. The dishes on the dinner menu were not ready yet, and this was the only available alternative—a special order offered to customers at this time of the day. From the way Vera was picking and poking absentmindedly at the food, it was clear that she was not convinced by the words of the man. In contrast to her obvious discomfort, the man seemed in a great optimistic mood, devouring his meal with gusto.

"*Personal matter*"..."*My business*"...*He is going to blow the entire situation...Poor me!* She sighed. Startled, the man raised his eyes from the fork and knife sinking into the soft kashkaval.[33]

"What's the matter?" he asked.

"Nothing. Nothing at all!" Vera said as she placed her fork and knife on her plate and reached for her purse. Suddenly, she had felt overcome by the uncontrollable craving for a cigarette.

§

It was about a year earlier when Vera had met Ricardo. It was in the bar at the casino in the Golden Sands resort. It was another darkened

---

32 *Cara mia* (Ital.)—my dear.

33 kashkaval (Bul.)—yellow cheese.

place, but full of people. It was noisy, and the air was thick with cigarette smoke. It was an accidental meeting of two strangers perched on high stools that lined a counter, with a view of rows of all shapes of bottles full of booze. Somehow this chance meeting turned into a relationship built on memories of early morning walks by the seashore; lazy afternoons spent under wide umbrellas stretched on chaise longue chairs, clad in colorful swimming suits and drinking lemonade; and, of course, romantic evenings. Sounds too good to be true, but sometimes such miracles happen. Vera was not just going through a process of healing, but a transformation. Born again, or whatever you want to call it, she was full of newfound hope and optimism. And it was with good reason.

Ricardo was a good man and single. A rarity in her life experience.

A couple of weeks at the Golden Sands passed quickly. Vera went to the airport to send him off and wave at the plane taking him away from her to his foreign country. The parting was not terribly emotional. As a matter of fact, Vera thought that this was the last she would see of him, and that all she would have left of him would be a bunch of pictures in a drawer. She was pleasantly surprised to get a letter from him only a short while after the airplane took him away. And that was the beginning of intense correspondence. Six months later, he was back, and he made his intentions clear. And they were serious ones. Vera decided that it was safe as well as necessary to take him to her parents. She couldn't imagine her father going to a restaurant to meet a man with serious intentions regarding his daughter. So Vera had to take him to her parents' place in the house on the corner. Because her parents' quarters were on the parterre, it was easy to make sure that she could sneak him inside without anyone seeing him, as well as minimize the possibility of Ricardo getting a whiff of the problem associated with contact with Westerners. And it was very naïve to imagine that Ricardo could pass for a local.

The visit was a success in every possible way. Vera's parents were truly impressed with the suitor, so much that her mother had a hard time keeping her happy mood under control and her mouth shut from blabbering and spreading the good news. Ricardo was also content with the prospect of having a traditional, modest couple for in-laws—strictly for the sake of his traditional, modest relatives back in his country. At least this was the impression he was left with from Vera's mother and father. And here ends the easy part of the love story.

According to the rules, marriage of a local to a Western foreigner was possible only if the wedding ceremony was performed in the native country of the local. It was an impossibility for more than one reason, though, so Vera and Ricardo had no choice but to get married in Vera's country. There was no objection on either side, so preparations were being initiated. However, it was expected by the couple that Vera would be going to live in Italy after the marriage occurred. Documents had to be collected, in some cases prepared, and permissions had to be given. It was taking much longer than Ricardo had anticipated. But he took it in stride. At one point in time, he received an unexpected phone call in his room in Hotel Bulgaria. It was a short message requiring him to show up in the early afternoon in a couple of days from the present at the entrance of Moskovska 5 and to ask for Comrade BC. The voice on the other end of the line was speaking in Italian and delivered his reassurances to Mr. Ricardo Ferrara that there would not be any problems regarding linguistic differences. He was to come alone.

The day was bright and sunny. The distance from his hotel to the place he was directed to go to was a few minutes away, a pleasant walk. He arrived on time, which was a very big thing for a man like himself, used to the leisurely rhythm of daily activities. However, he had been made to understand that there were rules and regulations here that had to be adhered to, and that in the situation he was in now, he should be very vigilant. There was a lot at stake, requiring for him to be on good terms with the authorities. It seemed that Ricardo had taken the advice seriously.

The building located at Moskovska 5, with its architecture of simplicity, uniformity, and clean geometrical shapes, sparkled under the sun rays reflected by the white polished stones and rows of glass windows covering its façade. It inspired a feeling as friendly as any administrative building can do, and then some. At the entrance, Ricardo was met by a stone-faced uniformed comrade seated in a cubicle behind a glass window. Shortly, a young male in civilian clothes appeared from the interior. Politely but unceremoniously and in perfect Italian, he informed Ricardo that he was a translator and would be assisting him in the communications. Then he turned abruptly and strode ahead. Ricardo followed him along a windowless corridor leading to a flight of stairs going downstairs, then through another windowless corridor, and finally to a windowless room with a desk occupied by Comrade BC. On the wall behind Comrade BC's chair hung a portrait of a man Ricardo had never seen a picture of. Anywhere.

From that moment on the interpreter became invisible. It was a miracle.

There was not a single piece of paper, a pencil, or any of the usual paraphernalia covering the desks of clerks or any other type of official. The effect this peculiarity of the setup of Comrade BC's desk had on Ricardo was extraordinary. It let him believe that this must be very routine business or even a situation created by mistake. In a very short while, he would be out of this windowless place that had made him feel a tinge of claustrophobia and even some weird feeling of dread. And just as Ricardo was ready to stand up and shake hands before leaving, Comrade BC started asking questions: "What is your name?"; "May I see your passport?"; "On what business are you here?"; and then, "How did you meet Vera Ivanova?"—omitting the official appellation of *Comrade* preceding each name. Meanwhile, Comrade BC had pulled out one of the desk drawers and taken out a bunch of small paper leaves on which he wrote the answers Ricardo was giving him. And he was doing it in a strange manner: Each answer was written on one of the small individual pieces of paper and pushed away to the far corner of the desk in a dismissive way. During the time Ricardo spent describing his meeting with Vera Ivanova, Comrade BC was staring at him with blank eyes. As the interpreter's voice went silent at the end of the short recitation by Ricardo describing the place and circumstances, Comrade BC pursed his lips, and Ricardo was startled to discern the sound of a faint sigh. After a pause portentous with bad news to come, Comrade BC opened the drawer from which he had taken the small papers, scooped them all in his hand, and put them back in the same drawer. Consequently, he closed this drawer, twisted his torso in the opposite direction, and reached to the drawer on that side. He pulled a paper file out of that drawer and placed it on top of his desk. Then he delivered a short speech.

"Mr. Ricardo Ferrara, this file contains information about Vera Ivanova the government of the Democratic Republic of BG would like you to know. We think that it is important for you to know what kind of person you are trying to marry. It is important to us also that people like Vera Ivanova do not end up going to other countries, where they might be regarded as a symbol of our country and its people."

Then Comrade BC opened the file and started reading, page after a page, a litany of names, places, and deeds associated with Vera Ivanova, all collected from reliable sources, none of which was mentioned. It took a while for the entire file to be read and translated to Ricardo. There were the names of a number of predominantly married men with whom Vera had had affairs, there was the incident of her attempted suicide, and there was other gossip collected over many years. Clearly this was a woman with a dubious reputation, mentally unstable and untrustworthy. Comrade BC had closed the file and set his piercing eyes on

Ricardo's face, waiting for the dramatic reaction. Ricardo, on the other hand, was displaying an increasing disinterest.

"Well, none of this has anything to do with my relationship with Miss Vera Ivanova. And I don't think that it should prevent us from getting married," he said nonchalantly. He shook Comrade BC's hand and left under the escort of the interpreter, who had become visible all of a sudden.

Back on the street, Ricardo took a deep breath and headed to his hotel. There were too many pressing, urgent matters to be taken care of before the fast-approaching date of the marriage ceremony. It was late afternoon and he was getting hungry, having missed his lunch.

"Hello, *cara mia*! Can you come to the hotel in half an hour? At the beerhall. For a bite and to tell you about an interesting meeting I had today..." Ricardo said on the telephone inside his hotel room.

"Yes, *mon cher*.[34] I'll be there. See you soon," Vera chirped cheerfully from the other end of the connection. A half an hour later they were sharing kashkaval-pane with fried potatoes on the side in the beerhall of Restaurant Bulgaria.

§

The wedding went as planned. There was a lot of palpable, demonstrative happiness in the air. Vera was radiant in her white suit Ricardo had brought from Milano for the occasion. It fit her perfectly too. It was amazing how well he knew the curves of her body...But I am digressing.

A short honeymoon followed in the resort by the Black Sea, the place where it all started. Roberto took a plane back home from the airport in the capital city. Vera came to send him away, to wave after the aircraft as it took off from the tarmac, and then returned to the house

---

34 *mon cher* (Fr.)—my darling.

on the corner to stay and wait until all the paperwork necessary for issuing an external passport was done. She looked radiant. Her parents were ecstatic, and the neighbors pretended to be. Normal. The only place for making and receiving telephone calls to or from abroad was the post office. Fortunately for Vera, there was one right on the corner of the closest intersection of the street on which the house on the corner was located. Every couple of days, Vera would go inside the large hall with its floor covered in marble, register for a call at the counter separating the clerks from the clients, take a seat on one of the benches, and spend an hour or so waiting for an empty cabin to become available. Making the connection required the assistance of several operators. And the wait would end with just a few minutes of conversation with Roberto. In no time her entire life was transformed; reduced to endless rounds of in and out through the doors of the post office and the telephone booth. The physical go-round was accompanied by a growing yo-yo state of emotions.

More time was passing. Roberto was complaining about the lack of progress regarding the issuing of Vera's passport. The officials in the Italian institutions were helpless. Their aggravation over the hopeless situation was apparent in the increased intensity of their gesticulations and the elevated pitch of their voices accompanying the delivery of all that bad news.

At one point in time, Roberto took time off his work and dropped by in the capital city of his wife, Vera, to try to understand what the problem was. What was going on? An official from the passport department told him—unofficially—that it was up to Moskovska 5. Roberto asked for advice, and he was told that the only feasible solution was for Roberto to move to Sofia. It came as a shock to all concerned. It seemed that nobody—nobody—had ever had such a thought cross his or her mind. Ever. Roberto flew back. Vera sent him off at the airport. She waved at the plane as it took off from the tarmac. It was out of habit.

A couple of years went by. During this time, Roberto came back for visits during his summer holidays and the two spent time at the resort by the Black Sea. Also, he had kept inquiring about the case of his wife's passport. Following his last inquiry, Roberto was told—unofficially— by the authorities in the passport department that the last delay was due to some new information received by the authorities from Moskovska 5. It was serious. There were new facts concerning Vera's parents' past. It had some connection to the events of 1947 and the trial of Nikola Petkov. Comrade Ivanov had somehow slipped through the cracks and avoided paying the price he should have paid, as all Enemies of the People did and would do in the future should they veer from the pre-scribed path. All of this was very confidential information and had been collected from a number of reliable sources. The original source was from one of the tenants living in the house on the corner. It was based on a rumor that someone from this address was involved somehow in the case of Nikola Petkov. It was also backed by information sent by trusted sources reporting from abroad—far away. There were some discrepancies regarding the floor where the traitors were living—the top versus the bottom floor—as well as the small matter of the names. No similarity whatsoever. But individual names mean little when the matter concerns the welfare of society against the deeds of evil individuals: the Enemies of the People. And anyone can change his or her name, no?

Vera filed for divorce immediately after the unofficial information was delivered to Roberto. The divorce was quick, and there weren't any complications. Roberto flew away for the last time from the airport of the capital city. Vera was there to wave as the plane took off from the tarmac for the last time. Miraculously, the rumors went away, and no more unofficial reports surfaced to raise further investigations. Vera went into a physical decline. The expression of her eyes had changed. Again. They lost their direct, confident, determined quality. The look in her eyes was of a scared doe, of a rabbit caught on the highway in the headlights of a car, running for her life. Her jaw had sagged and was drooping. Her cigarette addiction was there to stay. "*Poor me*," she kept moaning…

Ends to Tie, or Where Do We Go from There?

It was 1995. By then the world had changed. And Vera had gone through a transformation. Again. And it was for the better. She had never remarried. A few years earlier, she had established contact and kept in touch with her old friend Nedah, who had ended up in a country far, far away, even farther than Italy. Vera's parents had passed away a couple of years back, and she had become a pensioner at the age of fifty-five, as required by the law in her country regarding women. Unfortunately for her, she had no grandchildren to take care of, as it had become the norm there. So she had nothing to brag about either, but in spite of that, she felt at peace. And some good fortune befell her, as her friend, Nedah, invited her to accompany her on a trip to South Africa—all expenses paid by her, of course. Vera was overjoyed and happy to accept the invitation. Moreover, now she could get a passport without any problems. So she did.

The two met in Milano, Italy, on separate flights each took from her respective place of residence. The rest of the journey they continued together. At one point during a tour of some famous caves, Nedah heard someone speaking their native language and got agitated. It was quite understandable, Vera thought, but as far as she was concerned, she would have stayed away and pretended that she had nothing to do with any of those people.

Anyway, there was more to the story, but as far as Vera was concerned, this was enough attention she could spare in talking to or about these type of people…

The *more to the story* reference relates to her younger brother, Michael, or Misho, as he was called. As a start, it should be said that the relationship between the two siblings was not close. Partially this could be explained by the age difference, and the rest was due to all the gossip surrounding his sister Vera. To insulate himself from all that, he built a wall around himself. In a way, it had a positive outcome. He concentrated his efforts on his studies, and sports. The latter was mainly for finding an alternative environment for making friends. There was this shining moment of expectations during the time Vera got first married to Ricardo, but it turned into a nightmare at the end and precipitated the events following the demise of the marriage and the long-term developments in Misho's life.

Vera's parents were crushed by worries about their young son's future, and rightfully so. How would the *unofficial new information* affect his prospects for the near future? Would there be a problem with his application for enrolling in university, acquiring a higher education? The Ivanovs' concerns went even further, encompassing his future *professional development*, a euphemism for the now redundant word *career*—a remnant of the capitalistic past, suggestive of greed and exploitation. This also added to Vera's frustrations and her subsequent transformation. Thankfully, the rumors regarding the political transgression of Comrade Ivanov went away, and Misho did not suffer any harmful consequences stemming from the unsuccessful affair and marriage of his sister Vera. Of course, his parents never recovered from the shock and never relaxed until the end of their lives.

It was 1990 when Misho boarded a plane from Czechoslovakia (do you remember this country?) full of young and not-so-young but predominantly male passengers and took off to Cuba. After a long flight across the ocean, the plane landed at the airport at Gander, in the province of Newfoundland, for a scheduled refill of fuel. At the time of take-off, for the last leg of the flight, the plane was almost empty. The explanation for the extraordinary situation was simple. Most of the passengers had changed their minds regarding the final destination of their trip. It took a while till Vera got any news from her brother. He was fine and needed some documents—would she be able to send them to the following address? Yes, Vera wrote back. She would be able and willing, for she had found out that their old friend with whom they shared more than a toilet in the house on the corner was living in this part of the woods. And this is how it came to pass, the rest of the story…

Part Three

A Flash of Memory...

The weather was awful. It was the coldest, the snowiest, and the most depressing winter of the last quarter of a century, as I remembered. At the moment, I was standing at the window overlooking the street: desolate, empty of human or motor traffic, except for a singular figure of unidentifiable gender bundled from head to toe in layers of clothing and scarves, and wearing unisex shoes. A small fluffy pooch covered in a bright red sweater was running nearby, energetically shoving his nose in the snow, going forth and back, pulling on the leash held by its master. The light snow falling from the leaden gray sky was twirling around, blown by the wind. I could hear the sounds coming from the television set in the next room—the voice of the reporter, the alternating noises of a slogan-chanting crowd, the cacophony of background clatter including a prayer chant. It had been going on for hours. Crimea. Getting tired of the bleak picture in front of me, I returned to the television and fixed my gaze on the wide screen.

The reporter shown standing in the forefront holding the microphone kept craning his neck to take a look at the scene behind his back, anxiously. Heavily armed soldiers tightly bunched together, with faces covered with masks, were standing at the ready—Russians, according to the reporter—the uniforms were without identifying insignias. Behind were military vehicles without plates, according to the reporter.

The scene brought memories. Unsettling, bad ones. Old ones. Fifty years old. So vivid and stubborn. It felt like nothing had changed in such

a long time, even though things had been happening. But it was all part
of the same old story—at least this is how it feels for those who had
lived through the war.

It was springtime in Berlin, 1965. I was on my first visit to the city,
specifically, to East Berlin, on the east side of the Wall across the mythical place on the west side of it.

There were a couple of more days left for the duration of the trip
I had been on there. The following day was the one I was most excited
about—the forthcoming concert of Luis Armstrong. As it happened,
a small group of compatriots of mine had organized themselves and
purchased tickets for the event. The Embassy had been involved in that
initiative, as usual. Of course. All showed up for the performance early,
took their seats in pumped mood, and kept looking around with bright
eyes and giddy expressions on their faces proclaiming to the world tri-
umphantly that they had arrived. To see and hear the Great Satchmo!
Someone from the mythical world on the other side of the Wall. A
memory to pass on to their children and grandchildren...

West Berlin and the Convenience of Following Orders

A Couple of Months Later

S tanding on top of the bed, at the corner between the narrow wall and close to the sink located below the window facing the street running off the Konstantinstrase, Nedah stared at the door's handle as it rotated slowly downward, almost imperceptibly, without emitting as much as a squeak. The sparsely furnished room was barely wide enough for a single bed and a sink along one of its walls, and sufficiently long to accommodate the length of the single bed with some space left for a small table. The room was located at the end of a dingy corridor in the isolated corner of a sprawling apartment turned into a boarding house. Its size and location suggested that its original designation was as maid's room, once upon a time, before the war. At present, it was the cheapest accommodation affordable to poor Easterners engaged in shady businesses. A bed, a sink, and a table with a single chair pushed underneath it represented all the needed essentials for such a traveler. Nedah's suitcase, resting on the table's surface, left just enough space for spreading a single person's meal or a pad of writing paper.

A few minutes earlier, Nedah had heard the faint sound of muffled steps cease abruptly at her door. She had felt the muscles of her neck tense up; her breathing slowed and deepened while she tried to suppress the sound of it. She had slid her stiff body out of the covers on her bed and pulled herself up and back until she ended up standing straight with her back against the wall—trapped—with no place left to move farther away, staring at the door handle. The lever had stopped in a vertical position as the inside bar had reached the end of its stroke. The slight sound of shuffling and pushing on the wood passed; the door did not budge. Nedah closed her eyes and fell to the bed with a sigh of relief. The door was locked! It was hard to remember all she had to do at each moment, at each step, to keep safe. The concern about safety, the vigilance, the confusion, kept her brain on fire.

The handle went back to its horizontal position, then went down, and again…Then came the whisper, "Open the door." The voice was male. The accent wasn't German. But what did she know about accents? She stood up again. She threw a glance at the window. The street outside was dark. Very dark. It was also too low—two stories below the room level.

"Open the door," said the hissing voice, drifting in again.

"Go away!" she hissed back.

"Open the door," the voice repeated in Russian. But the accent was not Russian.

Time was passing. She kept her silence.

Finally, the sound of steps going away drifted through the closed door. Nedah stretched her arm to the sink, placed her hand under the tap, turned it on, and scooped a handful of water to splash on her face and neck.

The way to the communal bathroom from Nedah's room led to the end of the narrow corridor, passed by a couple of doors along the left wall, and ended after a turn to the right and into the reception area. It was early on the next morning when Nedah emerged from her room, still in her pajamas and bare feet, carefully sneaking along, hugging a large towel to her chest. As she reached the second door on the left of her room, bright sunlight flooded the dimly lit hallway, to be obscured immediately by the silhouette of a female figure emerging from the interior. She halted in expectation of Nedah.

"Come inside," the woman said curtly. She turned around and headed for a large armchair situated by the window. Nedah followed. She had seen the woman and was left with the impression that she was the manager.

"Sit down," the woman said, pointing to the low ottoman in front of the large chair before depositing herself in it. She spoke in a mixture of German and broken English in a sharp and commanding tone of voice. Presently, she produced a pair of silk stockings from a table drawer next to her chair and handed them to Nedah. Through a combination of verbal instructions and gestures, she proceeded to deliver a string of orders directed at Nedah, who was crouching at her feet. Nedah took the soft pile of material in her hand, following the commands in total disbelief and with a growing sense of fearful panic. The woman lifted her foot and placed it on Nedah's lap. Then she motioned that she wanted her stocking pulled up her leg.

"Last night you had a visitor," she said. Nedah kept her head low as she continued pulling one of the stockings over the woman's leg. *This is not happening to me. This must be just a bad dream…She knows this man. He must be living here.* She felt a strange sensation take hold of her head, in her brain, akin to fear and anxiety. The woman kept talking. "You never change your outfits. What do you keep in your suitcase?"

One leg was done. Nedah took it off her lap and brought the other foot, the bare one, in its place. The woman's body swayed a bit as she grabbed the handles of the armchair to steady herself. Meanwhile, she kept talking. "You should get some new clothes…"

The other leg was done and Nedah took it off, put it on the floor, pushed the low stool away, and stood up. The woman set her eyes on

Nedah—empty and cold. *She doesn't look German,* Nedah thought. *Polish maybe?* It made no sense. But then, this was West Berlin, and very little made sense in this island of affluence in the middle of the gray and miserable world outside the wall surrounding it. Standing straight in front of the chair, looking down at the bitter, worn-out woman, Nedah's anxiety and fear dissipated, and the only feeling left was a sort of pity. She turned around, picked up the large towel she had dropped by the low ottoman, and left the room.

It had been raining when Anne had reached Alexandre Plaza an hour ago, in the Eastern Zone of Berlin. At the crossing, she had produced her diplomatic passport for the official. She had withstood the usual scrutinizing stare and moved slowly away toward the train platform. The drive to the Zoo station on the other side of the wall was a short one, and it took her less than half an hour to get there. The rain had stopped, and she decided to walk to the designated meeting with Nedah. It was early afternoon, and she had an entire afternoon to spend away from the drab reality on the other side—although she had to make sure to cross the border and get back in the apartment before her father returned from his office to the place he now called home. She cherished those escapades, spoiled only by the danger of someone recognizing her, informing on her, jeopardizing her father's position.

The wide boulevard of Konfurstendame was lined with stores displaying all kinds of beautiful, desirable, and tempting merchandise. An enormous placard hung high on the wall of a newly constructed building at an angle that made the fantastic images of James Bond in action hard to miss from far away; the handsome face and the gun he held in a most unthreatening way were charming and exciting. The iconic church left with the scars of being halfway bombed and finished in brilliant modern design evoked wonderment. The contrast with the pile of rubble left by the destruction caused at the same time as the ruins created in the

Alexanderpalza, on the other side, was confusing and almost incomprehensible to the newcomer.

She spotted Nedah standing on the corner of the crossroad, in front of the building in which she was residing. The moment their eyes met, Nedah dashed toward her.

"What's the matter?" Anne said. "Did anything happen?"

"Never mind. I'll tell you later," Nedah blurted. "What are we going to do? Let's move away from here."

The apartment was small and crowded with furniture. The older lady opening the door seemed startled; it looked to Nedah as if it was her presence that caused the reaction. As a matter of fact, this entire trip was just as unexpected to her as it was to the somber-looking, somewhat faded frau standing at the door. As usual, Nedah had not asked questions, letting Anne drag her along on her errands. The explanations always followed, and that was all right, as far as Nedah was concerned. Once inside the parlor, all sat down, and an awkward silence followed for a brief period, all on the account of Nedah's presence, it seemed to her. There was a sense of uneasiness until Anne pulled an envelope from her purse and passed it to the woman. Meanwhile, a younger female had entered the room and quietly taken the seat close to the older one. The latter immediately ripped the envelope open, pulled the paper from its interior, and started reading it with full concentration. A few minutes later she finished reading and placed the paper back in the envelope, and a conversation between her and Anne followed. It was in German, and thus practically incomprehensible to Nedah. About an hour elapsed before Anne got up from her chair, took the package the older woman handed her, and motioned to Nedah that it was time to leave.

"This is the mother and the sister of a guy I met in the Eastern part," Anne said. "He used to live here with his parents and sister, but worked in the Russian zone and got caught on the other side when the Wall was built," Anne continued. "I bring letters to his relatives and carry some provisions back to him once in a while, when I come here." She ended her explanation with a glance at Nedah.

"Let me see your ring," she blurted, fixing her gaze on the ring on Nedah's left-hand middle finger, which she was turning around absentmindedly.

"Quite pretty. Unusual," she said while examining it, once Nedah had placed it in her hand.

"Can you help me sell it? I need the money…" Nedah whispered.

"Well, I have never done that, but we can try."

The shop window was sparsely decorated with sparkling jewelry placed on stands covered in velvet. Nedah and Anne stood on the sidewalk outside the store, gazing through the glass at the variety of bracelets, earrings, men's cufflinks, pins, and rings made of silver and gold, dazzled.

"Shall we go in?" Anne asked. Nedah nodded.

The shopkeeper standing behind the counter looked at the women with curiosity. A short conversation ensued. A few steps aside from Anne, Nedah kept her distance, staring at a point on the wall behind the proprietor, until she heard Anne's voice. "Pass me the ring." With some difficulty, she pulled it from her finger again and put in her friend's palm. The hemisphere of golden filigree shone with the reflected light of the afternoon sun.

"*Wunderbar*,"[35] the shopkeeper said as he took the ring from Anne's hand. After brief scrutiny, he put it back in the palm of her hand.

"Decent fellow," Anne muttered as soon as both exited the store and halted on the sidewalk in front of the shop window, while Nedah was pushing the ring back up her finger. The shopkeeper was clearly visible

---

35 wunderbar (Ger.)—wonderful.

through the glass, maintaining the same posture behind the counter, following the two women with an intense stare. Nedah felt the bout of nervous shivers go through her body. She heard Anne's voice talking to her.

"He said that the ring was handmade and it would be a mistake to sell it. You would not be able to get what it is worth."

"Oh…How so? The rings in the window look better…" Nedah blurted.

"Machine made," Anne snapped. The hint of contempt in her voice for such ignorance was unmistakable.

"So what?" Nedah snapped back.

The man seated at the reception desk kept his eyes glued to Nedah, following her every movement, straining his ears to catch a recognizable word or phrase coming from her lips as she spoke into the mouthpiece of the telephone she was clutching with both hands, her fingers wrapped tightly around the handle. The countenance of his face was frozen into a pleasant smile. A couple of days before, Nedah had approached his desk and handed him a package. It was a small piece of blue cheese with its seal broken.

"Would you accept this?" Nedah had managed to construct a short sentence in broken English as she handed the package to the man she knew as the receptionist. He looked at her, startled. She continued haltingly, "I bought this from the store thinking that it was something I have eaten. I have never tried it, but it must be good…It was expensive and I do not feel like throwing it away…"

The man's face had brightened as he took the package and read the label.

"You are right. It is expensive, and I love it." He kept looking at her with a smile that grew brighter and wider, while Nedah's bewilderment deepened and feeling of regret took hold of her. Then she had turned around and disappeared into the dark hallway leading to her room. Today she had come back to his desk and asked if she could use the telephone. She could, the man had said with smile—friendly and conveying intense curiosity; she seemed to be oblivious to the reason. At the conclusion of her phone call followed by a curt "*Danke*," she scurried toward her room. Inside, she picked up a bag she had prepared a couple of days before, locked the door on her way out, and hurriedly proceeded to the staircase.

The U-Bahn[36] was moving fast, and the rhythmic sound of the wheels penetrated the interior of the empty coupé. The bag containing a bottle of Pliska cognac sat on the empty seat next to Nedah, who kept constant pressure on the curved surface applied by the palm of her hand placed on top of it. She was convinced that stopping the bottle from rolling away, getting damaged, and spilling its contents at every turn of the direction of the train's movement and the jerks at each acceleration or deceleration was essential to the success of her mission. Occasionally she would pull out a small pocket-sized book with her free hand, struggle to open it, glance at the address scribbled on it, and take a look outside at the fast-moving panorama behind the glass as though checking on the progress of her trip—useless exercises by all means, but something that helped her keep her mind busy while gripped by excruciating anxiety. A young woman in her early twenties met her at the station and led her to a car parked close by. It was a white Mercedes no more than a couple of years old. At the end of a short ride, the car came to a stop in front of a low decorative fence of manicured evergreen bushes.

The interior of the house was cozy. Light music drifted from a large living room furnished with sensible, comfortable furniture. The twilight

---

36 U-Bahn (Ger.)—rapid transit underground railway in Berlin, the capital city of Germany.

of a late-spring day penetrated through the windows, creating an ambiance of calm and peacefulness. Nedah stood in the middle of the room, still holding the bag in her hand, staring through the window, immersed in the feeling of safety, until a muffled sound of steps of someone moving carefully over the floor partially covered with a Persian rug made her turn her head in the direction of its origin. A young man carrying a silver plate covered with refreshments was headed toward the low round table surrounded by the low sofa and armchairs covered in pastel-colored damask with a floral motif. His eyes, cast down, never moved away from the tray, his steps sure and quiet as of a walking ghost. His olive skin and thin limbs suggested that the young man was not a local, and most probably of a Middle Eastern origin. In awkward silence, Nedah observed his movement while standing in the middle of the room. An older stately man accompanied by a middle-aged woman walked into the room as soon as the young man with the now empty tray hanging from his arm disappeared into the darkness of the interior. Suddenly Nedah felt comfortable, relieved.

"Hello. I am Nedah. Here is the letter from your friend, and here is something from me," she said as she handed the bag containing the letter and the bottle of Pliska cognac to the lady of the house. The conversation was in her native tongue. The story was of a German man married to a native of a country he used to do business with before the war. The accent aside, his command of the foreign language was impressive. The young girl who had picked up Nedah at the station was their daughter. Obviously she understood everything, but kept her silence.

An hour later all four were seated around the table covered with a white tablecloth and a display of elegant tableware. The polite conversation was only occasionally interrupted to allow the young man to serve a course or take away dishes from the previous one. The menu was simple and sensible—like everything else, including the company, Nedah thought.

"Our daughter is attending school right now. Tourist management," the man said. "She is planning on continuing her education in London. Do you have any plans for the future?" he added, changing the subject.

"Yes. I would like to go far away, possibly America…"

"Great idea," the man said, quickly erasing the hint of a smirk on his face caused by surprise or whatnot. "Good idea indeed. That would have been my choice if I was still a young man, of course. It is the continent of opportunities, for sure," he concluded authoritatively.

At the end of the evening, standing by the open outside door, shaking hands, the middle-aged lady of the house turned toward Nedah. "Have a safe journey back," she said. "Give us a call when you arrive at the hotel." After a short drive to the U-Bahn station she had disembarked at a few hours earlier, Nedah got out of the beautiful white Mercedes and boarded the U-Bahn train, making her way back to the hotel.

Unsettled by the middle-aged woman's words, she kept asking herself all the way till she got off the train and completed her journey home—on foot, trotting and skipping along: "What did she mean by wishing me a safe journey?" On her arrival at the hotel, she went straight to the reception desk and asked for the telephone.

"Hello!" she was surprised to hear herself screaming. "Thanks for the pleasant evening." She paused. "No, had no problems whatsoever." Another pause. "Thank you again. Good night." Hardly able to conceal the resentment in her voice from the guy behind the desk, she turned around and rushed to her room, locked the door, and sat on the bed without taking off her overcoat. The faint noise drifting from the street slowly took over her. Another day was over. Just another day of wandering…lost…

I want to go home. The darkness and the heavy worry are descending over me, throwing a deep shadow of fear on my mind, taking away the bright shine of hope and expectations. I want to go back to the security of the inertia and resignation. I feel tired, worn out. I am writing a letter. I am pleading to be told to go back home. It is a cowardly gesture, but I have no strength left for heroism anymore.

A week later I get an answer. It is written in code that we had developed before I left. It seems that the code had worked. The coded message is short and leaves no doubt: "Do not come back!" There is no explanation. It is an order, clear and concise. I feel a huge relief. The bigger the challenge, the stiffer the determination! Following orders is best, though. It is the way we've been brought up how to survive.

Epilogue

Random Thoughts...

The date of my last death and resurrection event was February 25, 2015. The exact time and place of its occurrence was at 8:15 a.m. in the bathroom adjacent to our master bedroom. It happened after one of my bad, sleepless nights that had ended with a peaceful medically induced morning snooze that, in its turn, had ended in a relatively cheerful awakening. As I stood in front of the mirror, staring at my pasty face and messy hair, I was overwhelmed by the old feeling that I have experienced previously on few occasions during my life.

This year is a special one for me. It is half a century since I left one world behind to start a new life in a new world I knew little of but have embraced as an alternative to the bad one I knew enough of. The very day this happened was also the day that marks the beginning of those reoccurring death and resurrection events of my life that always take place after long periods of a life spent in the twilight zone. What I mean is to say that from then on, there was light at the end of the tunnel that was absent in the days before, in the old world.

Actually, this latest episode must have been triggered by the new, fresh postings I'd seen on the Internet regarding the most recent disclosures concerning the *secrets of the past* published in a newspaper in the motherland. And that meant a quick trip back into the twilight.

Well, I shouldn't have been so surprised at the news I have been hearing a lot about, trickling slowly in drips and drops over the last twenty-plus years, and I believe that I have come to terms with all that. It is water under the bridge, I reason. But the nagging doubts and bitter thoughts come back to haunt me…

And one final thought on the matter of the light at the end of the tunnel…

A life lived in the asylum of one's mind, surrounded by many memories, overwhelming thoughts, and creeping, unwelcome revelations about life itself, creates its own morality. But it takes time to build that new set of rules without shattering the old fundamental codes, standards, and beliefs installed in us in the dawn of our earthly existence. And that calls for reexamination and reevaluation of one's life. Maybe it will even open some of the hidden doors built in the walls of the asylum and let liberation happen. I hope.

But, I am digressing…

Echoes of the Literary Circle

It is a late afternoon of a hot summer day slowly coming to its end. The sky is blue and the sun has moved to the west. The shadows from the trees have grown long. The downtown is undergoing a kind of a metamorphosis, when the city starts shedding the mantle of oppressive heat that had kept its inhabitances inside, creating the eerie picture of an abandoned place with its lonely streets and apartment buildings with tightly closed windows and empty balconies. It is the time when the streets start to fill with traffic and the gardens with pensioners tightly squeezing close to one another as they try to utilize the long shadows thrown by all the trees over the benches. The noise of the streetcars passing by mixed with children's joyous screams and loud whines produces a cacophony of constantly varying intensity. It hadn't changed a bit in the many years I was away. And neither had my affection for the moment and the city at that moment...

It was one of those times and in a slightly different setting when I found myself sitting at a table under an open sun umbrella surrounded by old classmates. It is a restaurant in the backyard of an apartment building close to the house on the corner. I was told that this gathering is, in fact, a tradition established soon after most had graduated from the university or simply settled down with families, raising children, and building careers. One of them had kept in touch and now took me there. It was a surprise. And it felt awkward. The silence was screaming at me. *Foreigner.* Someone had brought a small child. Apparently all knew the youngster, and he knew them all. So he fixed his eyes on me: the stranger. He had beautiful, innocent eyes. A hint of a smile was taking shape on the features of his face. "What is your name?" I asked.

"Ivan," he said. Suddenly he added, "Where are you from?"

All eyes were on me. I just didn't know what to say.

"From the house on the corner," I finally ventured.

"What house are you talking about?" he asked with eyes wide open, staring me down.

"What do you mean? Don't you know the house on the corner?"

But before I could say anything more, a voice laden with impatience snapped at me.

"There is no more house on the corner. It was taken down about twenty years ago, and a new apartment building is standing in its place now. If you are interested, I could take you there and show it to you."

"Thanks, but no thanks," I snapped back. I was so sure that I saw the house from the corner of my eye. Later on, I apologized, and the rest of the get-together went smoothly.

At one point in time, I started to feel discomfort. It was the type of feeling that someone is watching you. It came from a direction I had accidently glanced in earlier, where a couple of men were sitting and talking with one another. I didn't recognize either, so I moved my eyes from them and did not look back till this moment. One of the men was staring at me. As soon as our eyes met, he stood up from his chair and dragged it all the way to my chair. Unceremoniously, he turned to the person seated next to me and said, "Just move away. Make room for my chair."

The woman got up, grabbed her chair, and dragged it away from my chair, opening enough space for the guy to squeeze his next to mine. She never stopped talking to whomever she was talking to before and never took her eyes off the person she was having the conversation with.

"You don't remember me, but I remember you," the man said. "My brother, he was older than me, was a member of the Literary Circle, and I used to attend sometimes. De facto,"[37] he continued, "I became a member later on." He smiled. "As a matter of fact, I became a writer and published a few books. Wonder if you would be interested to read some of them?"

"Sure," I said.

Suddenly a loud voice drifted from behind us. It was the voice of the woman who sat next to me.

---

37 De facto (Latin)—in fact.

"Hey! What have you been doing lately? Traveling abroad?" she said as she wrapped her arms around the neck of the man from the Literary Circle as she bent over him. "What happened to your good manners? Just pushing me out of my place without a simple *please?*"

Then she laid an affectionate kiss on his cheek and started to rock him in her embrace. The man kept smiling.

I just stood up and walked away, looking for someone to start a conversation with, while murmuring "de facto" under my breath. From the corner of my eye, I saw the woman releasing the man from her embrace, pushing away my chair and pulling hers next to him. Both were laughing. *Thank goodness, I am not missed.* The thought crossed my mind.

At the end of my vacation in the motherland, I met with the guy from our get-together at the beginning of my visit in the country. We met in a café in the downtown area, but far away from what I remembered as the house on the corner. He arrived with a bag full of books. We had a long and very interesting conversation, but not exactly like the ones we had at the meetings of the Literary Circle. At the end of our meeting, we shook hands like old friends; I took the bag full of books and waved back after we said our good-byes and each took on a different direction.

Meanwhile, Farther Away, Inside the Land of the Sunflower Seeds...

Another place in the old country. Another late summer afternoon when the heat has subsided. The earliest signs of the evening hubbub to follow are showing in the first wave of customers starting to drift in the patios in front of dingy restaurants or simply old garages converted into a variety of mini-shops. The enterprising proprietors—people with big dreams and limited means—had set a couple of tables surrounded by pairs of chairs on the sidewalk in front of their establishments, where people took a seat to drink the coffee they had purchased inside the garage/shop and carried to the outside.

And before dusk another sight to behold is leisurely being assembled, composed of the older citizens appearing from the smelly, dirty interiors of the panel apartment buildings with crumbling walls and balconies with rows of wash-lines full of clothes and their esthetically unpleasing usage as storage spaces for some strange and some standard household objects. The benches lining the walls on the ground level are filling up with people. Old and older ones.

The conversations are lively but not absorbing. It is clear by the shifting eyes and cranking necks of the observers following each passerby. The only absorbing activity is the incessant spitting and cracking of the sunflower seeds by each individual holding a bag of the stuff in one hand while, with rhythmic and absentminded movements, emptying it by poking the fingers of his other hand into it. The activity carried out by the old is shared by the young ones occupying the patios close by. If nothing else, this is the one impression that a stranger would take away from that scene. It could be assumed that it would be one of a unified people with a common mind-set, regardless of age—except for a teenager locked up in the room on the eighth floor in one of the apartments, clearly distinguishable by the fresh pink color of the recently installed thermal isolation panels, a newly introduced method by the EU to help reduce heating cost. It is called *sanirane*.[38] The girl is sitting in her shorts, surrounded by the sound of the latest hit songs performed by Taylor Swift, hunched over an English grammar manual, readying

---

38 sanirane (Bulg.)—a technology for thermal insulation of buildings.

herself for the realization of a *dream come true* under the sharp supervision of her determined grandmother. Part of a journey as grand and full of adventure as the *Odyssey* but with a different destination: *England*. But I am digressing again…

…And the Old Man in the Village Abandoned by the Birds

He had just stepped out of the door and was about to close the screen door behind his back when he felt the pleasant sensation of the caress of a late-spring breeze on his face and heard the barely audible sound of rusty chain links rubbing against one another's surfaces right above his head. He cranked his head and raised his eyes to the old wooden sign hanging under the protrusion over the entrance. He glanced at the sign "Nightingale" and let it linger for a while in a state of a sudden realization at the thought that something was wrong. It was the absence of the sweet sound of the mating chirpings of the nightingales so familiar during this time of the year. As though from nowhere, another observation felt a couple of days ago came to his mind: the absence of late of the haunting sound produced by the large tree branches rubbing their bark one against another at the occasional rush of wind. The mighty oak spreading its enormous crown in a most domineering way over the small brook was missing. Gone. The old man had already heard the rumors and seen some of the consequences of the actions of the culprit responsible for all the devastation. Suddenly he felt the rush of a moist feeling in his eyes. The absurdity of the sign emptied of its meaning hit him hard. The old oak tree, the habitat for the nightingales, had been hacked mercilessly. The birds had gone away. And so had the granddaughters of the neighbor. Gone to a place far, far way, to a foreign country their grandfather had hated before and now embraced.

Gently the man pulled the door closed, hesitating for a moment about what to do next—all of his original intentions forgotten at the thoughts that had suddenly overwhelmed him. Finally, he dragged his feet along the shady wall, deposited himself on the weathered old wooden bench pushed next to the stucco covering the façade of the house, and rested his clasped hands in his lap. There was not an ounce of strength that he was able to muster to wipe the tears slowly streaming down the skin of his tawny cheeks.